Outstanding Monozukuri Companies *in Japan*

Narumi Yoshino

Justin Harris

Osamu Inoue

Paul Leeming

SHOHAKUSHA

はじめに 謝辞にかえて

　大学生向け英語リーディングテキスト、『知られざる日本の「ものづくり」企業の世界』をお届けします。

　2018年3月初旬。執筆メンバーが数年間あたため続けてきた、「ものづくり」に躍進する日本企業を特集した英語教材の作成企画に向けて、協力企業を探すことになりました。

　突然お電話をして、各社広報ご担当者様を驚かせてしまったかもしれません。にもかかわらず、本企画について説明の機会を与えて頂き、社内でのご検討の末、最終的にご快諾を頂戴した12社で教材化への第一歩を踏み出すことができました。

　ここに、各企業の窓口となって頂いた皆様を掲載章順にご紹介します。

　植月真一郎様（マツダ・1章、5章、15章）、中田和毅様（ハウス食品・2章）、山崎明子様（TOTO・3章、15章）、仲西美沙希様（シマノ・4章、15章）、山岸裕欣様（京滋マツダ・5章後半）、池川優太様（UCC上島珈琲・6章、15章）、榎本明子様（ダイフク・7章）、井上さゆり様（サクラクレパス・8章）、岩本絵里奈様（ヤンマー・9章、10章、15章）、沖本美貴様（オタフクソース・11章、15章）、安原誠様と佐藤望様（トンボ学生服・12章）、西村恵美様（日東電工・13章）、そして栢由起子様（モロゾフ・14章）、以上14名の方々です。

　ご担当の皆様には、情報提供へのご協力に始まり、社内での原稿確認作業の陣頭指揮、貴重な画像のご提供等々、大変お世話になりました。お忙しい中、多くの方々が各章冒頭の企業紹介文をご寄稿下さったことも、ここでお礼を申し上げておかなければならないでしょう。また、社史にお詳しいご担当者様からは、メディア向けの特別な情報を頂きましたし、事業内容や製品の成り立ちについて、熱心にご説明くださった方も多数いらっしゃいました。ご所属企業について、正しく、より詳しく、学生たちに伝えたいという皆様の職務に対する強い責任感と、善意のお気持ちに支えられ、本書はここに完成いたしました。ご担当者皆様のご尽力と、頂いたご縁に心より感謝申し上げます。

　本書で取り上げる企業は、第二次世界大戦の戦禍をくぐりぬけ、戦後の復興を経て今日まで約80年から150年の歴史を誇っています。また、その製品はどれも、明治以降日本が輸入に頼らざるを得なかった西洋のものを自分たちの手で作りだそうというところから生まれ、今日「ものづくり」精神の粋を極めるに至ったものばかりです。日本の近現代史と共に歩んできた12社について、全国の大学生が英語学習を通して学び、日本が世界に誇る「ものづくり」の伝統とその高い技術力に思いを馳せてくれることを願います。

　最後に、本教科書出版にあたり、ご尽力頂きました松柏社の永野啓子様、心を一つに、志を同じくして本企画を進められたことを何より幸運に思います。ありがとうございました。

　　　　　　　　　　　　　　　　　　　　　2019年春　近畿大学東大阪キャンパスにて
　　　　　　　　　　　　　　　　　　　　　執筆者代表　吉野成美

Contents

Chapter 1   6

マツダ
- 広島から世界へ
——挑戦と開発の一世紀

Chapter 2   14

ハウス食品
- 西洋の味を食卓に
——食を通じて人とつながる

Chapter 3   22

TOTO
- トイレと、ともに。
——快適な水まわりを創造する

Chapter 4   30

シマノ
- もっと自然へ、もっと人へ。
——自転車文化と釣り文化の創造

Chapter 5 特集記事   38

マツダデザイン
- クルマはアート——
造形美と新たなるブランドの構築へ

Chapter 6   46

UCC上島珈琲
- 「カップから農園まで」
——世界唯一のコーヒーカンパニー

Chapter 7   54

ダイフク
- マテハンの世界へようこそ
——進化する物流ソリューション

Chapter 8   62

サクラクレパス
- 走れ、クレパス列車
——子供たちに「彩り」をとどけて

Chapter 9　　　　70

ヤンマー
■ 小さなものから大きなものまで
　──テクノロジーで拓く豊かな未来

Chapter 10　特集記事　78

山岡孫吉の生涯
■ 「燃料報国」への想い──
　小型ディーゼルエンジン開発物語

Chapter 11　　　　86

オタフクソース
■ 一滴一滴に性根を込めて
　──お好み焼を世界へ

Chapter 12　　　　94

トンボ学生服
■ 文化としての「制服」──最良の
　ユニフォームメーカーを目指して

Chapter 13　　　　102

日東電工
■ 見えない場所から世界を変える
　──グローバルニッチトップ™戦略

Chapter 14　　　　110

モロゾフ
■ バレンタインは神戸から
　──心に響く洋菓子の鐘

Chapter 15　特集記事　118

ミュージアムとカフェ
■ 歴史と製品に囲まれて
　──生み出されるわたしたちの未来

Chapter 1

Mazda
マツダ

企業紹介

マツダは、「走る歓び」を通して人生に輝きをもたらすことを目指している自動車メーカーです。およそ100年前に広島の地で生まれたマツダのクルマは今日では130カ国以上で販売され、2017年度の販売台数は160万台を数えています。2012年以降、魂動デザインと、走る歓びを犠牲にすることなく優れた環境・安全性能を提供するSKYACTIV技術を搭載した商品が世界中で幅広く受け入れられています。

Grammar Tips for the TOEIC® L&R Test

受動態に副詞が割り込む「be動詞＋副詞＋過去分詞」の語順を押さえておこう。

本文では以下の表現が見られます。

The SKYACTIV technology has been positively received by critics and consumers alike.

副詞 positively が、受動態「be動詞＋過去分詞」をつくっている been + received のあいだに割り込むような形で、動詞 receive を修飾しています。

例題を見てみましょう。

> The company's website is (　　) updated to add their press releases.
> 　(A) frequency
> 　(B) frequent
> 　(C) more frequent
> 　(D) frequently

ここでは、動詞 update を修飾する (D) の副詞 frequently を選択します。もちろん、updated 以下のかたまりを、分詞の形容詞的用法や分詞構文のかたまりとして考え、be動詞の補語として (A) の名詞や (B)・(C) の形容詞を選択できる可能性はありますが、ここでは文の意味が通じなくなります。

TOEIC® L&R では、文法問題で副詞が選択肢にあれば、**まず副詞を空欄に入れて考えてみて良い**ぐらい、副詞が正答となる文法問題のパターンが数多くあります。

Vocabulary Questions

以下の語句の意味を、下の語群から選びましょう。

1. achieve _____
2. aim _____
3. attempt _____
4. automobile _____
5. cause _____
6. completely _____
7. critic _____
8. experience _____
9. failure _____
10. government _____
11. headquarters _____
12. incredible _____
13. initially _____
14. part _____
15. positively _____
16. prize _____
17. realize _____
18. suggest _____
19. survive _____
20. vehicle _____

賞	部品	信じられない	〜を暗に示す
試み	本社	完全に	〜を実現する
経験	乗り物	最初は	〜を達成する
失敗	自動車	好意的に	〜を引き起こす
政府	評論家	生き残る	〜することを目指す

Language in Use 🔊 Audio 1-02

音声を聴いて空欄を埋めましょう。さらに、完成した文の日本語訳を下線部に書きましょう。

1. (　　　)(　　　)(　　　)(　　　), the new jeans they designed sold out quickly.

   _____

2. (　　　)(　　　)(　　　)(　　　), they will conduct a market survey of the new item.

   _____

3. They (　　　)(　　　)(　　　)(　　　) their customers satisfied with their products.

   _____

Mazda 7

Reading

1 The company that is now Mazda started in Hiroshima in 1920 as Toyo Cork Kogyo Co., Ltd. As the name suggests, it initially produced cork. In 1921, Jujiro Matsuda, the son of a fisherman from Hiroshima, who learned his professional skills in machinery in Osaka, took charge of the company. Following the depression after the Great Kanto Earthquake in 1923 and a serious fire in the factory in 1925, the company was in danger of bankruptcy. Jujiro even thought of moving to live in Brazil but reconsidered. As he was an expert in machinery, he decided to restart his business as a machine company. In 1927, the company dropped the word "cork" from its name and became Toyo Kogyo Co., Ltd.

2 In 1929, motorcycle racing was very popular in Japan. In order to produce its own three-wheeled truck, the company began by developing a motorcycle, which is similar to a three-wheeled truck. They wanted it to be completely Japanese made because in those days in Japan, most of the motorcycles were either imports or built with imported parts. In October 1930, Mazda's motorcycle, powered by a 250cc 2-stroke engine, entered a famous race in Hiroshima. To everyone's surprise, the motorcycle beat the famous British-made Ariel, and Mazda won the race on their very first attempt. Despite this incredible success story, Mazda has never made another motorcycle in their long history. After this, the company entered into the automobile industry, and it made a three-wheeled truck in 1931. This memorable first motor vehicle, called the Mazda-Go Type DA, was a big success and set the company on the path to worldwide fame.

3 On August the 6th, 1945, an atomic bomb was dropped on Hiroshima, causing widespread death and destruction. It happened to be Jujiro's birthday and, as was his tradition, he went for a morning haircut. The barber shop opened at 7:30, and Jujiro made sure he was the first there. He got a haircut, and 30 minutes later was in his car on the way to work. At 8:15, the bomb exploded almost right above the barber shop. If Jujiro had been a little late for the

barber, he would not have survived, and Mazda may never have gone on to become the world leader that it is today.

4 A small mountain shielded the factory and headquarters of Mazda, which were almost completely undamaged in the attack. Their buildings were used by the prefectural government as offices for almost a year following the bomb. Mazda recovered quickly and by the end of 1945 was producing three-wheeled trucks again.

5 Mazda has always aimed to be unique, and this can be seen most in their engines. In 1961, Mazda entered into a partnership with a German manufacturing company, NSU / Wankel, to produce the rotary engine, which combined high power with a very compact size.

Most companies considered the engine to be a pipe dream, and many tried to produce it and failed. It wasn't until 1967 when Mazda produced the rotary powered Cosmo Sport, that the dream was realized. The engineers had achieved the impossible through vision, perseverance, and persistence.

6 Keen to test the performance of their rotary engine, Mazda was involved in motor sports, and began with a Le Mans debut in 1974. Many failures followed, but Mazda did not give up, and 18 years later, in its 13th attempt, it won the Le Mans race in 1991, becoming the first Asian car maker to win this prize. Le Mans is a 24-hour race, and has been called the "Grand Prix of Endurance and Efficiency." By winning it with the rotary engine, Mazda showed its underlying character and determination to succeed.

7 With the same spirit that helped to perfect the rotary engine, Mazda has continued to work hard to develop its SKYACTIV technology. The SKYACTIV technology has been positively received by critics and consumers alike, and has won several Car of the Year awards. Mazda is determined to continue perfecting their technology to make our driving experience even better.

NOTES

◆ l. 2 Toyo Cork Kogyo Co., Ltd.　東洋コルク工業株式会社　◆ ll. 3-4 Jujiro Matsuda　松田重次郎　◆ l. 12 Toyo Kogyo Co., Ltd.　東洋工業株式会社　◆ l. 30 the Mazda-Go Type DA　マツダ号DA型　◆ ll. 51-52 NSU / Wankel　NSU・バンケル社　◆ l. 56 Cosmo Sport　コスモスポーツ　◆ l. 59 Le Mans　ル・マン24時間耐久レース　◆ l. 69 SKYACTIV　スカイアクティブ

1 Synonym Questions

以下の語句の同意語を選びましょう。単語の左側の数字はその語句が出てくる本文の段落番号です。

1. **1** suggest _____
2. **1** serious _____
3. **1** expert _____
4. **2** beat _____
5. **2** fame _____
6. **3** widespread _____
7. **4** shield _____
8. **5** achieve _____
9. **6** keen _____
10. **7** positively _____

defeat	favorably	reach	specialist	eager
imply	renown	extensive	protect	severe

2 Questions & Answers

質問の答えとして正しいものを一つ選びましょう。

1. Why did Jujiro Matsuda reconsider moving to live in Brazil?

    (A) Because he decided to restart the company.

    (B) Because the company was in danger of bankruptcy.

    (C) Because the Great Kanto Earthquake occurred.

2. Why did Mazda probably recover quickly right after the war?

    (A) Because Hiroshima Prefecture helped it recover.

    (B) Because the plant was saved from destruction.

    (C) Because three-wheeled trucks became a big success.

3. For what is Mazda most likely to continue working hard?

    (A) Completing its SKYACTIV technology

    (B) Getting more positive reviews and awards

    (C) Stopping production of the rotary engine

3 Comprehension Check

本文の内容に合うものを一つ選びましょう。

1. ①〜②段落に関して
   (A) As soon as the Mazda-Go Type DA began selling extremely well, Mazda became famous around the world.
   (B) Mazda entered motorcycle racing with a motorbike made with entirely domestically produced parts.
   (C) Mazda introduced one motorbike after another because it won a famous motorcycle race.
   (D) When Jujiro became president in 1921, the word "cork" had been removed from the name of the company.

2. ③〜④段落に関して
   (A) After getting his haircut, Jujiro went home to celebrate his birthday.
   (B) Jujiro made it a rule to have his hair cut on his birthday.
   (C) Mazda used the buildings of the government of Hiroshima as its headquarters.
   (D) The factory and headquarters of Mazda suffered great damage.

3. ⑤〜⑦段落に関して
   (A) Mazda produced the rotary engine in order to form a partnership with NSU / Wankel.
   (B) Mazda won the Le Mans race on their very first attempt, just as it had won the motorcycle race.
   (C) Most companies thought it impossible to produce a high-powered and compact-sized rotary engine.
   (D) The reviews of Mazda's SKYACTIV technology have been divided between critics and consumers.

4 Composition

あなたが興味をもっている企業についてホームページなどで事実を調べ、例文を参考にして以下の空欄にあてはまる語句を入れて、その企業の説明を英語でしてみましょう。参照する企業は、例文ごとに変えても、すべて同じ企業でもかまいません。

例1 In 1921, Jujiro Matsuda took charge of Toyo Cork Kogyo Co., Ltd.
1921年に松田重次郎は東洋コルク工業株式会社の代表となった。

企業名 _____
In (　　　　), (　　　　　) took charge of (　　　　　).

例2 Mazda entered into a partnership with a German manufacturing company to produce the rotary engine.
マツダはドイツの製造会社と提携し、ロータリーエンジンを製造した。

企業名 _____
(　　　　) entered into a partnership with (　　　　) to (　　　　).

例3 Mazda has won several Car of the Year awards.
マツダはいくつものカー・オブ・ザ・イヤー賞を獲得している。

企業名 _____
(　　　　) has won (　　　　) award(s).

2016 World Car Awards 授賞式

5 Chronological Table

本文の内容に基づいて、以下の年表を完成させましょう。

年　号	出　来　事
（①　　　）	東洋コルク工業株式会社として創立する。
1921 年	（②　　　　　）が社長に就任する。
（③　　　）	モーターバイクのレースで英国製バイクを抑えて優勝する。
1931 年	（④　　　　　）の生産を開始する。
（⑤　　　）	広島に原子爆弾が投下される。
	本社の建物の一部を（⑥　　　　　）に提供する。
1961 年	（⑦　　　　　）を開発するため、NSU／バンケル社と技術提携をする。
（⑧　　　）	（⑦　　　　　）搭載車である（⑨　　　　　）を発売する。
1991 年	（⑩　　　　　）でアジアのメーカーとして初めて優勝する。
現在	数多くの（⑪　　　　　）を受賞している。
	（⑫　　　　　）技術の完成へ向かって邁進している。

日本カー・オブ・ザ・イヤーを受賞した歴代のマツダ車

ファミリア（1980-1981）

カペラ（1982-1983）

ロードスター 3 代目（2005-2006）

CX-5（2012-2013）

デミオ（2014-2015）

ロードスター（2015-2016）とトロフィー

Chapter 2

House
ハウス食品

企業紹介

ハウス食品は、カレーやシチュー、スパイスやラーメンなどの製造・販売を主な事業活動としています。他にもスナック、デザート、介護食など、幅広い分野の製品を展開しています。創業者である浦上靖介の思いを現在に受け継ぎ、「食を通じて、家庭の幸せに役立つ」企業を目指して、これからも多岐にわたる製品で日本中の家庭に温かい家庭の味を届けることに貢献していきます。

Grammar Tips for the TOEIC® L&R Test

「冠詞＋副詞＋形容詞＋名詞」の語順を押さえておこう。

本文では以下の表現が見られます。

Tongari Corn has also become an incredibly well-known snack.

副詞 incredibly が直後の形容詞 well-known を修飾し、さらに、「副詞＋形容詞」の形容詞のかたまり incredibly well-known が直後の名詞 snack を修飾します。

TOEIC® L&R では、形容詞が過去分詞であるパターンが多く出題されます。

> The (　　) developed legal system in Japan is quite remarkable.
> (A) height
> (B) high
> (C) higher
> (D) highly

過去分詞 developed を修飾する (D) の副詞 highly を選択します。ここでは legal system が「形容詞＋名詞」のかたまりをつくり、それを「副詞＋形容詞」の形容詞のかたまりが修飾するという、やや複雑な構造になっています。

このパターンは、本文では以下の表現に見られます。

After some time people realized that they could not tell any difference in taste between expensive English imported curry, and the locally produced curry powder.

ここでも curry powder が「形容詞用法の名詞＋名詞」のかたまりをつくっています。

Vocabulary Questions

以下の語句の意味を、下の語群から選びましょう。

1. aid _____
2. analysis _____
3. (be) intended for _____
4. contain _____
5. diet _____
6. domestic _____
7. expand _____
8. launch _____
9. local _____
10. luxury _____
11. manufacturer _____
12. medicine _____
13. popularity _____
14. responsible _____
15. stack _____
16. storage _____
17. subsidiary _____
18. taste _____
19. transportation _____
20. win _____

味	子会社	国内の	～を助ける
薬	メーカー	地元の	～を獲得する
人気	輸送(機関)	功績がある	～を発売する
分析	ぜいたく品	拡大する	～を積み重ねる
保管	日常の食事	～を含む	～を対象としている

Language in Use

 Audio 1-04

音声を聴いて空欄を埋めましょう。さらに、完成した文の日本語訳を下線部に書きましょう。

1. Can you (　　　)(　　　)(　　　)(　　　) engine performance between the two cars?

   _____

2. The new off-road bike is (　　　)(　　　)(　　　)(　　　) to decide to buy without thinking first.

   _____

3. The history of that old establishment is (　　　)(　　　)(　　　)(　　　) of ours.

   _____

Reading

 Audio 1-05

1 Do you ever feel like eating curry for breakfast? When Ichiro Suzuki was playing for the Seattle Mariners, his breakfast on the day of every home game was Japanese curry. Was that the key to his amazing success? Either way, curry has become a large part of the Japanese diet, and
5 perhaps the company most responsible for this is House.

2 Initially House began life in 1913 as Urakami Shoten, a company dealing in herbal medicine. The company was established in Osaka by Seisuke Urakami, and moved into the curry business in 1926 with its Home
10 Curry brand. Originally, curry powder was imported from England, and was an expensive luxury, only  intended for rich families. Local companies began to make curry, and after some time people realized that they could not tell any difference in taste between expensive English
15 imported curry, and the locally produced curry powder. From this point, people became happy to use Japanese curry powder, and domestic manufacturers boomed.

3 In the 1950s, companies started making curry roux, a solid block type curry mix
20 that is still used today. However, perhaps the biggest revolution in the world of Japanese curry occurred in 1963, when House introduced its Vermont Curry. This curry mix contained apple and honey, and
25 was far sweeter and milder than other curries that were produced at that time. Until this point, curry had always been considered to be a dish for adults, and a little too spicy for children. Vermont Curry changed all of this and made curry a very popular dish for young children. Curry rice has been one of children's favorite school lunch dishes for the past 30 years.

30 **4** The company has produced other favorites with both children and adults, including Fruiche, which is a fruit-flavored dessert that was  introduced in 1976, and is perfect for the hot Japanese summer. Fruiche has enjoyed such great
35 popularity that if you stacked all the boxes ever sold on top of each other, the pile would be more than 142 km tall. That is more than

37 times the height of Mount Fuji. Tongari Corn was launched in 1978 and has also become an incredibly well-known snack.

5 House has continued to develop and expand, and is not limited to producing food. It has moved into the health food business, and in 2004 launched a new product called Ukon No Chikara, or "the power of turmeric." Turmeric is a root similar to ginger, and is said to aid digestion, and also to prevent hangovers.

In 2008, the company introduced its One Day Vitamin drink, with 13 vitamins that you need for one day provided in a single drink.

6 House is the largest producer of spices and a household name in Japan, but is also known around the world. In the early 1980s, House opened up a

subsidiary, House Foods America. The mission of the company was to introduce healthy Japanese food into the American diet, and although curry has become increasingly sought after, House is known in America for another healthy food — tofu. In fact, House is the leading provider of tofu in the whole of the U.S., with factories on the east and west coasts providing 350,000 blocks of tofu every day. Outside of the US, House is also doing business in China, Korea, Thailand, Indonesia, and other places around the world. In China, their curry mix is most in demand from customers, while in Thailand, C-vitt, a drink rich in vitamin C, is their main product. In Indonesia, they focus on producing Halal curry for food companies.

7 House has expanded all over the world, with its products winning affection and popularity both at home and abroad. The company is involved in other food-related businesses such as commercial food suppliers, transportation and storage, and even food safety and hygiene analysis.

NOTES

◆ l. 1 **Ichiro Suzuki**　イチロー（鈴木一朗）　◆ l. 6 **Urakami Shoten**　浦上商店　◆ l. 8 **Seisuke Urakami**　浦上靖介　◆ l. 55 **House Foods America**　ハウスフーズアメリカ　◆ l. 68 **Halal**　ハラール

1 Synonym Questions

以下の語句の同意語を選びましょう。単語の左側の数字はその語句が出てくる本文の段落番号です。

1. **1** amazing _____
2. **2** establish _____
3. **2** taste _____
4. **2** domestic _____
5. **3** point _____
6. **3** spicy _____
7. **4** perfect _____
8. **4** stack _____
9. **6** focus _____
10. **7** win _____

| achieve | flavor | ideal | pile | concentrate |
| found | moment | remarkable | hot | national |

2 Questions & Answers

質問の答えとして正しいものを一つ選びましょう。

1. In what way was Vermont Curry an epoch-making product?
    (A) It became a popular lunch dish with children.
    (B) It ended the notion that curry was a dish for adults.
    (C) It was the first solid block type curry mix in Japan.

2. What product is most likely to be taken the day after you drank too much?
    (A) Fruiche
    (B) One Day Vitamin
    (C) Ukon No Chikara

3. What is the main product House sells in China?
    (A) Curry mix
    (B) Tofu
    (C) Vitamin drinks

Comprehension Check

本文の内容に合うものを一つ選びましょう。

1. ①～②段落に関して

   (A) As soon as Urakami Shoten was established, the company set up the curry business.

   (B) Ichiro Suzuki ate Japanese curry for breakfast whenever he played baseball.

   (C) Japanese companies began to make curry powder, and people were immediately happy to use it.

   (D) Japanese people came to realize that curry powder made in Japan had almost the same taste as imports did.

2. ③～⑤段落に関して

   (A) Fruiche has been popular among children because adults don't like fruit-flavored desserts very much.

   (B) One Day Vitamin contains a substance made from a root like ginger as the main ingredient.

   (C) When House introduced its Vermont Curry, making curry sweeter and milder had become the main focus of the curry industry.

   (D) When you take Ukon No Chikara, it may prevent you suffering from indigestion.

3. ⑥～⑦段落に関して

   (A) Except for the U.S., House has been expanding its business only in Asian countries.

   (B) House Foods America supplies more tofu than any other company in the U.S.

   (C) House is drawing up plans for expansion into some new industrial sectors connected with the food industry.

   (D) The task that House's subsidiary in the U.S. had to fulfill was to open factories to produce tofu.

Composition

あなたが興味をもっている企業についてホームページなどで事実を調べ、例文を参考にして以下の空欄にあてはまる語句を入れて、その企業の説明を英語でしてみましょう。参照する企業は、例文ごとに変えても、すべて同じ企業でもかまいません。

例1 Initially, Urakami Shoten dealt in herbal medicine.
初めは浦上商店は薬草を扱っていた。

企業名 _____
Initially, (　　　　　) dealt in (　　　　　).

例2 House has moved into the health food business.
ハウスは健康食品事業に進出した。

企業名 _____
(　　　　　) has moved into the (　　　　　) business.

例3 House is the leading provider of tofu in the whole of the U.S.
ハウスはアメリカ全土で豆腐を供給しているトップクラスの会社だ。

企業名 _____
(　　　　　) is the leading provider of (　　　　　) in (　　　　　).

カリッとした食感が人気のとんがりコーン

Chronological Table

本文の内容に基づいて、以下の年表を完成させましょう。

年　号	出　来　事
1913 年	浦上靖介が大阪に（①　　　　　）を設立する。
（②　　　　）	薬草ビジネスから、（③　　　　　　）ビジネスに進出する。
1950 年代	（④　　　　　　）の開発を始める。
（⑤　　　　）	（⑥　　　　　）と（⑦　　　　　　）を使った「バーモントカレー」を発売する。
1976 年	夏にぴったりのデザートの（⑧　　　　　）を発売する。
（⑨　　　　）	人気スナック「とんがりコーン」を発売する。
1980 年代	アメリカに子会社（⑩　　　　　　）を設立する。
2004 年	（⑪　　　　　）ビジネスに進出し、「ウコンの力」を発売する。
現在	さまざまな（⑫　　　　　）ビジネスにも進出している。

バーモントカレー（甘口）の変遷

1963 年

1980 年

1989 年

1998 年

1995 年

現行のバーモントカレー（甘口）

Chapter 3

TOTO
TOTO

企業紹介

2017年に創立100周年を迎えたTOTOは、日本では下水道の概念さえ一般的ではなかった時代に、腰掛式水洗便器を製造しました。以来、「健康で文化的な生活を提供したい」という創立者、大倉和親の志を事業の根幹にすえ、挑戦と革新を繰り返し、今では日本の多くの家庭に普及しているWASHLET™をはじめとした様々な水まわり商品を生み出し、新たな生活文化を創造し続けています。

Grammar Tips for the TOEIC® L&R Test

助動詞と動詞の間に割り込む副詞、不定詞に割り込む副詞を押さえておこう。

本文では以下の表現が見られます。

① That is a complete bathroom set that can easily be fitted into a house.
② The modules became very popular as a way to easily install bathrooms in houses and apartments throughout Japan.

副詞 easily が、①では助動詞 can と動詞 be fitted のあいだに、②では不定詞 to install のあいだに、それぞれ割り込むように入っています。

例題を見てみましょう。

> The board of directors will (　) nominate Andrew for the head of the committee.
> 　(A) define
> 　(B) defining
> 　(C) definite
> 　(D) definitely

高校で学んだ5文型を振り返ってみると、副詞は基本的に文の主語・動詞・目的語・補語という文の主要素になることができない修飾語でした。しかし、副詞は修飾語でしかないからこそ、名詞も動詞も形容詞も入ることができない場所に入っていくことができるのです。ここでは、(A) の動詞はもちろん、(B) を動名詞や分詞と考えた名詞・形容詞も、(C) の形容詞（または名詞）も空欄に入ることができず、(D) の副詞が正答となります。

同様に、不定詞に割り込めるのは副詞だけです。

Vocabulary Questions

以下の語句の意味を、下の語群から選びましょう。

1. address _____
2. available _____
3. collect _____
4. consumption _____
5. development _____
6. engineer _____
7. establishment _____
8. general public _____
9. impressed _____
10. income _____
11. innovation _____
12. install _____
13. joint venture _____
14. laboratory _____
15. plumbing _____
16. reduce _____
17. remain _____
18. resources _____
19. respected _____
20. temperature _____

温度	収入	合弁会社	〜を集める
開発	消費	一般の人々	〜を減らす
革新	設立	利用できる	〜に取り組む
技師	配管	評価の高い	〜を設置する
資源	研究所	感銘を受けた	〜のままである

Language in Use

 Audio 1-06

音声を聴いて空欄を埋めましょう。さらに、完成した文の日本語訳を下線部に書きましょう。

1. The president discovered the value of a thing (　　　)(　　　)(　　　)(　　　).

   _____

2. The owner (　　　)(　　　)(　　　)(　　　) a sophisticated security system.

   _____

3. That company (　　　)(　　　)(　　　)(　　　) in solving the problem by rewriting the software.

   _____

Reading

 Audio 1-07

TOTO

1 Many people in the modern world take toilets for granted, but they are incredibly important in our life, and have made our environment cleaner and safer. We also spend a lot of time there! One recent poll showed that we might spend up to 100 days of our life on the toilet.

2 TOTO has been making ceramic sanitary ware for over a hundred years, and their constant high-quality innovations have brought them success. In an interview with *The New York Times*, the owner of an American plumbing company said that sitting on a toilet not made by TOTO would be like "going back to the Stone Age." So, how did TOTO become such a well-known and respected company? To find the answer, we have to go back to the beginning of the 20th century.

3 In 1903, while in Europe, Japanese businessman Kazuchika Okura was impressed by the ceramic seated flush toilets and other sanitary ware items that he found there. After returning to Japan in 1912, he established a ceramic sanitary ware laboratory within his company, Nippon Toki Gomei Kaisha. Soon after this, the company began to carry out research and development of sanitary ware. Then, in 1914, the company successfully developed Japan's first ceramic seated flush toilet. In 1917, Kazuchika established the "Toyo Toki Company" in Kokura, Fukuoka, which produced toilets and other sanitary ware items, such as wash basins.

4 A major innovation came in 1963. When the company had to equip the Hotel New Otani with bathroom units in a very short time to be ready for the Tokyo Olympic Games in 1964, it developed the "prefabricated bathroom module." That is a complete bathroom set that can easily be fitted into a house. The modules became very popular as a way to easily install bathrooms in houses and apartments throughout Japan.

5 From its initial establishment, the company has set its sights on the rest of the world. So, after changing its name to "Toto Kiki Ltd." in 1970, it began with a joint venture company in Indonesia in 1977. In 1990, the

establishment of a sales office in the United States led to TOTO's eventual success there, and the company has since expanded throughout China, other Asian countries, and Europe.

6 In 1980, TOTO introduced an amazing new innovation that changed toilets forever. The "WASHLET™" was a seat that could be attached to toilet bowls. It allowed users to wash with warm water. It took engineers a long time with trial and error to perfect the WASHLET™. With no data available, around 300 employees at the company helped them to collect it by testing out different water temperatures and different angles for the water. Finally, they found the perfect water temperature and the best angle for the water to come out. The angle was 43 degrees, which has remained the same for all subsequent products.

7 WASHLET™ equipped toilets were first used by high income earners. This amazing innovation eventually spread to the general public in Japan, and has started to become known around the world. By 2015, TOTO had sold 40 million units!

8 TOTO is also proving to be innovative in their ecological business model. They are a company that is committed to addressing environmental problems. In 2014, TOTO set a number of "TOTO Global Environmental Vision" goals. These goals seek to improve water conservation, conserve natural resources, and help to prevent further global warming, among other things. For example, one of TOTO's goals is to reduce water consumption from flushing the toilet. Some toilets use up to 10 liters of water or more for one single flush. Presently, TOTO has refined the technology for water-saving, and now many of their toilets use less than four liters per flush.

9 With the combination of their technological innovation and environmental focus, TOTO is sure to enjoy continued growth in the 21st century.

NOTES

◆ l. 16 Kazuchika Okura 大倉和親 ◆ l. 20 Nippon Toki Gomei Kaisha 日本陶器合名会社 ◆ ll. 25-26 Toyo Toki Company 東洋陶器株式会社 ◆ l. 37 Toto Kiki Ltd. 東陶機器株式会社 ◆ ll. 63-64 TOTO Global Environmental Vision TOTOグローバル環境ビジョン

1 Synonym Questions

以下の語句の同意語を選びましょう。単語の左側の数字はその語句が出てくる本文の段落番号です。

1. **1** poll　　　　＿＿＿＿＿＿＿
2. **3** produce　　＿＿＿＿＿＿＿
3. **4** install　　＿＿＿＿＿＿＿
4. **5** establishment ＿＿＿＿＿＿＿
5. **6** collect　　＿＿＿＿＿＿＿

6. **6** remain　　＿＿＿＿＿＿＿
7. **7** income　　＿＿＿＿＿＿＿
8. **8** address　　＿＿＿＿＿＿＿
9. **8** refine　　＿＿＿＿＿＿＿
10. **9** growth　　＿＿＿＿＿＿＿

| development | gather | place | tackle | earnings |
| improve | stay | foundation | manufacture | survey |

2 Questions & Answers

質問の答えとして正しいものを一つ選びましょう。

1. What did TOTO do in 1963?

    (A) It asked Hotel New Otani to install TOTO bathroom units.

    (B) It enabled Hotel New Otani to develop a complete bathroom set.

    (C) It helped Hotel New Otani to be ready for a big sporting event.

2. What has TOTO hoped to do since its foundation?

    (A) To advance into foreign markets with its products

    (B) To develop Japan's first ceramic seated flush toilet

    (C) To introduce a major innovation in the industry

3. What is true about the WASHLET™?

    (A) It changed the established concept of toilets.

    (B) It was developed for high income earners.

    (C) Its data were secret and not available.

Comprehension Check

本文の内容に合うものを一つ選びましょう。

1. ①〜②段落に関して
   (A) According to a recently conducted survey, everyone is likely to spend up to 100 days sitting on the toilet from now on.
   (B) Many people today believe that toilets play a very important role in modern life.
   (C) The owner of a U.S. plumbing company said to an interviewer that he wished there had been TOTO toilets in the old days.
   (D) TOTO's success is attributed to the fact that it has constantly made new high-quality products.

2. ③〜⑤段落に関して
   (A) After coming back from Europe, Kazuchika Okura established Nippon Toki Gomei Kaisha.
   (B) Starting a joint venture in Indonesia was used as an opportunity to change its name to Toto Kiki Ltd.
   (C) The establishment of the Toyo Toki Company followed the development of Japan's first ceramic seated flush toilet.
   (D) TOTO's eventual success in the U.S. resulted in the foundation of a sales office there.

3. ⑥〜⑨段落に関して
   (A) Engineers at TOTO smoothly completed the WASHLET™ with help from its employees.
   (B) The best angle for water to come out has changed since the WASHLET™ was introduced.
   (C) TOTO is planning to combine its innovative technology with its focus on the environment in the future.
   (D) TOTO's toilets save more than half the amount of water per flush of some other toilets.

4 Composition

あなたが興味をもっている企業についてホームページなどで事実を調べ、例文を参考にして以下の空欄にあてはまる語句を入れて、その企業の説明を英語でしてみましょう。参照する企業は、例文ごとに変えても、すべて同じ企業でもかまいません。

例1 TOTO has been making ceramic sanitary ware for over a hundred years.
TOTO は 100 年以上にわたって衛生陶器を製造し続けている。

企業名 _____
(   ) has been making (   ) for (   ) years.

例2 In 1914, TOTO successfully developed Japan's first ceramic seated flush toilet.
1914 年に TOTO は日本初の陶製腰掛水洗便器を開発することに成功した。

企業名 _____
In (   ), (   ) successfully developed (   )'s first (   ).

例3 By 2015, TOTO had sold 40 million units of the WASHLET™.
2015 年までに TOTO は 4 千万台のウォシュレット(※)を販売した。

企業名 _____
By (   ), (   ) had sold (   ).

※「ウォシュレット」は TOTO の登録商標です。

Chapter 3 TOTO

5 Chronological Table

本文の内容に基づいて、以下の年表を完成させましょう。

年　号	出　来　事
（①　　　）	ヨーロッパで（②　　　　　　）が衛生陶器に感銘を受ける。
（③　　　）	（②　　　　　　）が日本陶器合名会社内に製陶研究所を設ける。
（④　　　）	日本初の陶製腰掛水洗便器を完成させる。
1917年	福岡県北九州市の小倉に（⑤　　　　　）を設立する。
1963年	簡単に設置ができる（⑥　　　　　）を開発する。
（⑦　　　）	社名を東陶機器株式会社に変更する。
1977年	（⑧　　　　　）に合弁会社を設立する。
（⑨　　　）	トイレの概念を変える新商品（⑩　　　　　）を発売する。
1990年	（⑪　　　　　）に販売拠点を設立する。
（⑫　　　）	この年までに4千万台の（⑩　　　　　）を販売する。
現在	技術革新とともに環境への取り組みをしながら、発展を続けている。

洗面化粧台「オクターブ」

システムキッチン「ザ・クラッソ」

システムバスルーム「シンラ」

Chapter 4

Shimano
シマノ

企業紹介
1921 年、大阪・堺で創業したシマノは、アウトドア・スポーツを代表するサイクリングと釣りの 2 つの分野を中心に、様々な製品を展開しています。使う人の感性に応えられるような「こころ躍る」製品を提供するため、常に時代の先端を行く「技術開発」「製品開発」に取り組んでいます。

Grammar Tips for the TOEIC® L&R Test

「be 動詞＋副詞＋形容詞」の語順を押さえておこう。

本文では以下の表現が見られます。

Although the company is now incredibly successful, its beginnings were more humble.

形容詞 successful が be 動詞 is の補語となっており、その形容詞を副詞 incredibly が修飾しています。

例題を見てみましょう。

> The machine the company developed is extremely (　　) in harvesting grains.
> (A) efficiencies
> (B) efficiency
> (C) efficient
> (D) efficiently

ここでは、be 動詞 is の補語となる (C) の形容詞 efficient を選択します。be 動詞の補語を選ぶという観点からは、(A)・(B) の名詞も正答の候補となるでしょう。もちろん the machine と efficiency では意味が結び付かないということもありますが、それよりも大きな「名詞を選択しない」理由は、空欄の前に副詞 extremely があることです。
副詞が名詞や代名詞を修飾することもないわけではありませんが、動詞・形容詞・副詞を修飾するのが本来の機能です。したがって、ここでは、be 動詞の補語のはたらきをしていて、しかも副詞に修飾されている形容詞 efficient を選択することになります。

Vocabulary Questions

以下の語句の意味を、下の語群から選びましょう。

1. amazing _____
2. competition _____
3. component _____
4. contribute to _____
5. currently _____
6. depend on _____
7. develop _____
8. different _____
9. division _____
10. international _____
11. leading _____
12. location _____
13. operation _____
14. participant _____
15. promote _____
16. range _____
17. recent _____
18. rent _____
19. steadily _____
20. supply _____

操作	参加者	さまざまな	〜を開発する
部品	一流の	現在	〜を供給する
部門	最近の	着実に	〜を促進する
場所	驚くべき	及ぶ	〜を賃借する
競技会	国際的な	〜に貢献する	〜しだいである

Language in Use

🔊 Audio 1-08

音声を聴いて空欄を埋めましょう。さらに、完成した文の日本語訳を下線部に書きましょう。

1. The machine (　　　)(　　　)(　　　)(　　　) (　　　) the item in large numbers.

   _____

2. The 19th (　　　)(　　　)(　　　)(　　　)(　　　) the Industrial Revolution in Europe.

   _____

3. The CEO (　　　)(　　　)(　　　)(　　　)(　　　) the major papers every morning.

   _____

Reading

🔊 Audio 1-09 SHIMANO

1 What do you think of when you hear the name Shimano? Depending on your hobby, you may think of fishing tackle, or bicycle components, and Shimano is a world leader in both. You may never have bought something directly from Shimano, but you probably can't ride a bicycle without using components that it has made. Shimano supplies high-quality and high-performance components for different types of bicycles, ranging from bicycles for the world's top racers to daily users.

2 Shimano is a company with a very long history, beginning in 1921 when at the age of just 26, Shozaburo Shimano opened Shimano Iron Works in Sakai City, in the south of Osaka. Although the company is now incredibly successful, its beginnings were more humble, with Shozaburo renting a small factory 40-square meters in size, for just five yen a month. In this factory, Shozaburo had only one machine and it wasn't his own — a lathe which he borrowed from a friend. When he started, he already knew what he wanted to manufacture — freewheels. It is one of the hardest bicycle components to manufacture, and this is what Shozaburo decided to focus on.

3 The company steadily grew in size, and in 1940 Shimano Iron Works Co., Ltd. was established. By this stage there were about 300 employees, and Shozaburo Shimano became the first company president. Shimano progressed and continually developed new products, including its external gear changer which started production in 1956, and an internal speed changer (internal 3-speed Hub) in the following year. The internal speed changer was then displayed for the first time at the International Toy and Cycle Show held in New York City in 1961. Bicycle sales in the United States were brisk, and the company established Shimano American Corporation in New York City in 1965.

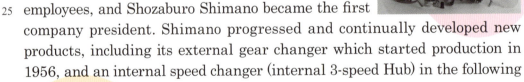

4 In 1973, the company launched forged aluminium cranks, which were employed in the first generation of their DURA-ACE series. This series is Shimano's flagship component in the road racing world. More recent

32 Chapter 4

developments include the Dual Control Lever that was released in 1990. This lever enabled the rider to perform shifting and braking operations with a single lever without releasing their hand from the handlebar. This mechanism triggered a revolution in road racing.

5 Shimano is not just a manufacturer of bicycle components. In 1970, the company established a fishing tackle division as another part of its business. The following year saw the introduction of the DUX series of spinning reels. Currently, Shimano is widely considered to be one of the leading manufacturers of fishing tackle in the world.

6 As a company that develops, produces, and sells bicycle components and fishing tackle, Shimano contributes to promoting health and happiness by encouraging outdoor activities related to these areas. It organizes the Shimano Suzuka Road, the road race event, which is held in August every year. Beginning in 1984, it is now one of Japan's largest road racing events, held annually at the International Racing Course in Suzuka Circuit, with a total of about 12,000 participants. Another event that also started in 1984, is a fishing competition called the Shimano Japan Cup. Currently, tournaments in several fishing categories are held in various locations across Japan throughout the year.

7 Shimano has continued to grow, and now has factories and offices around the world, including Uruguay in South America, and Cambodia in South East Asia. That is quite amazing for a company that started in a small factory with one lathe borrowed from a friend. Next time you ride your bicycle, take a look at the different components. How many of them are Shimano?

NOTES

◆ l. 11 Shozaburo Shimano　島野庄三郎　◆ l. 11 Shimano Iron Works　島野鐵工所　◆ l. 19 freewheel　フリーホイール　◆ l. 23 Shimano Iron Works Co., Ltd.　株式会社島野鉄工所　◆ l. 27 external gear changer　外装変速機　◆ l. 28 internal speed changer (internal 3-speed Hub)　内装変速機（3スピード・ハブ）　◆ l. 33 Shimano American Corporation　シマノアメリカンコーポレーション　◆ ll. 35-36 forged aluminium cranks　アルミ鍛造クランク　◆ l. 37 DURA-ACE series　DURA-ACEシリーズ　◆ l. 39 the Dual Control Lever　デュアルコントロールレバー　◆ l. 47 the DUX series　DUXシリーズ

1 Synonym Questions

以下の語句の同意語を選びましょう。単語の左側の数字はその語句が出てくる本文の段落番号です。

1. **1** component _____
2. **1** different _____
3. **2** rent _____
4. **3** steadily _____
5. **3** progress _____
6. **3** brisk _____
7. **4** release _____
8. **5** division _____
9. **5** currently _____
10. **5** leading _____

| active | develop | major | various | constantly |
| launch | nowadays | department | lease | part |

2 Questions & Answers

質問の答えとして正しいものを一つ選びましょう。

1. What did Shimano begin to produce in 1957?
   (A) An external gear changer
   (B) An internal speed changer
   (C) Freewheels

2. What is true about the Shimano Japan Cup?
   (A) It is divided into several sections.
   (B) It is held annually in Suzuka City.
   (C) It is held in several places on the same day.

3. What is true about the history of Shimano?
   (A) It has continued producing bicycle parts and fishing tackle since it was established.
   (B) Shozaburo's small factory was rented, but he owned some pieces of machinery.
   (C) The DUX series was released before the DURA-ACE series.

Comprehension Check

本文の内容に合うものを一つ選びましょう。

1. ①〜②段落に関して
   (A) Shimano is a leading company in the world market for fishing tackle and bicycles.
   (B) Shimano's products are of such high quality and performance that they aren't suited to general use.
   (C) Though he opened a factory, Shozaburo was at a loss about what to make first.
   (D) When Shozaburo started his business, its operations were conducted on a very small scale.

2. ③〜④段落に関して
   (A) After Shimano opened an office in the United States, bicycle sales there briskly increased.
   (B) Shimano's DURA-ACE series once dominated the road racing world as its flagship component.
   (C) Shimano's external gear changer was exhibited at an international fair held in New York City.
   (D) The development of the Dual Control Lever led to a dramatic change in road racing.

3. ⑤〜⑦段落に関して
   (A) As it doesn't have a long history in the field, Shimano's fishing tackle division has been having a hard time.
   (B) Participants in Shimano's fishing contest move around Japan for several years to become the overall champion.
   (C) Shimano has arranged some outdoor events for a long time.
   (D) Shimano's fishing tackle division took a few years to launch its first product.

Composition

あなたが興味をもっている企業についてホームページなどで事実を調べ、例文を参考にして以下の空欄にあてはまる語句を入れて、その企業の説明を英語でしてみましょう。参照する企業は、例文ごとに変えても、すべて同じ企業でもかまいません。

例1 At the age of just 26, Shozaburo Shimano opened Shimano Iron Works in Sakai City, in the south of Osaka.
26歳のとき、島野庄三郎は大阪南部の堺市で島野鐵工所を開設した。

企業名 _____
At the age of (　　　), (　　　) opened (　　　) in (　　　).

例2 In 1970, Shimano established a fishing tackle division.
1970年にシマノは釣具事業部を設立した。

企業名 _____
In (　　　), (　　　) established a (　　　) division.

例3 Shimano organizes the Shimano Suzuka Road and the Shimano Japan Cup.
シマノはシマノ鈴鹿ロードとシマノジャパンカップを主催している。

企業名 _____
(　　　) organizes (　　　).

Chronological Table

本文の内容に基づいて、以下の年表を完成させましょう。

年　号	出　来　事
1921 年	（①　　　　　　　）が大阪府堺市で島野鐵工所を開く。
（②　　　）	株式会社島野鉄工所となり、（①　　　　　　）が初代社長となる。
（③　　　）	外装式変速機の生産を始める。
（④　　　）	内装式変速機（3 スピードハブ）の生産を始める。
（⑤　　　）	ニューヨークにシマノアメリカンコーポレーションを設立する。
1970 年	自転車部品の製造にとどまらず、（⑥　　　　　）を設立する。
（⑦　　　）	スピニングリール（⑧　　　　　　）シリーズを発売する。
（⑨　　　）	アルミ鍛造クランクを開発し、ロードレース界におけるシマノの旗艦製品となっている（⑩　　　　　　）の初代シリーズで使用される。
1984 年	シマノが主催する（⑪　　　　　　）と、（⑫　　　　　　）が始まる。
1990 年	ハンドルから手を離すことなく（⑬　　　　　　）操作と（⑭　　　　　　）操作ができる（⑮　　　　　　）を開発する。
現在	世界中に工場と事業所があり、発展を続けている。

自転車に乗らない人からサイクリング愛好家まで魅了するシマノサイクリングワールド（シンガポール）

好奇心を大切にし、カフェやアートイベントなど、新しい自転車の愉しみ方を提案するライフ・クリエイション・スペース OVE（オーブ）（東京都港区）

Chapter 5

Mazda Design
特集記事 マツダデザイン

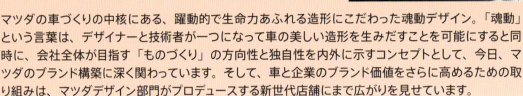

マツダ VISION COUPE デザインスケッチ

マツダの車づくりの中核にある、躍動的で生命力あふれる造形にこだわった魂動デザイン。「魂動」という言葉は、デザイナーと技術者が一つになって車の美しい造形を生みだすことを可能にすると同時に、会社全体が目指す「ものづくり」の方向性と独自性を内外に示すコンセプトとして、今日、マツダのブランド構築に深く関わっています。そして、車と企業のブランド価値をさらに高めるための取り組みは、マツダデザイン部門がプロデュースする新世代店舗にまで広がりを見せています。

Grammar Tips for the TOEIC® L&R Test

not only A but also B, both A and B, either A or B, neither A nor B は頻出する。

本文では以下の表現が見られます。

① **For many people, a car is not just a means of transport, but is also a fashion item.**
② **Everything is designed meticulously to ensure that both the cars on display and the space itself create the perfect atmosphere.**

①では not only (= just) A but (also) B が、②では both A and B が用いられています。

例題を見てみましょう。

> Proficiency in (　) English and Spanish is one of the requirements for the job.
>   (A) both
>   (B) either
>   (C) neither
>   (D) nor

ここでは、空欄のあとにある and をキーワードに (A) の both を選択します。みなさんがよく知っている、both A and B, either A or B, neither A nor B, not only A but also B は好んで出題される文法事項ですので、例題のようにフレーズ内のキーワードから正答を導きましょう。

Vocabulary Questions

以下の語句の意味を、下の語群から選びましょう。

1. atmosphere　_____
2. attract　_____
3. aware　_____
4. common　_____
5. compromise　_____
6. ensure　_____
7. evident　_____
8. expect　_____
9. fulfill　_____
10. function　_____
11. ideal　_____
12. launch　_____
13. mechanic　_____
14. on display　_____
15. outlet　_____
16. practical　_____
17. process　_____
18. reflect　_____
19. response　_____
20. supervision　_____

開始	返答	実際の	〜を満たす
過程	整備士	明らかな	〜を期待する
監督	販売店	気づいて	〜を反映する
機能	雰囲気	理想的な	〜を引きつける
妥協	共通の	陳列されて	〜を確実にする

Language in Use

🔊 Audio 1-10

音声を聴いて空欄を埋めましょう。さらに、完成した文の日本語訳を下線部に書きましょう。

1. The CEO (　　　)(　　　)(　　　) the serious risks the company is now taking.

　_____

2. (　　　)(　　　)(　　　) the matters we have discussed, we need a bold strategy.

　_____

3. They (　　　)(　　　)(　　　) between the two measures after long negotiations.

　_____

Reading

マツダミュージアム内展示のR360

1 For many people, a car is not just a means of transport, but is also a fashion item, reflecting their taste and sense of style. Mazda is aware of this, and its focus on design is evident from their very first passenger car, the Mazda R360, launched in 1960. For Mazda, the idea of motion is central, and since the launch of the Zoom-Zoom brand in 2002, the company has focused on more athletic and sporty cars.

2 Since 2010, Mazda has introduced a new concept for the design of their cars — 'KODO: Soul of Motion.' This continues the company's focus on movement, and is based particularly on the beauty of animal movement. Ikuo Maeda, the then head of Mazda's Design Division, explains, "To sum up what we mean by KODO Design, it's about creating cars that embody the dynamic beauty of life; cars that visually suggest different expressions of this energy. In Japan, we feel that craftspeople inject life into what they make, so objects that receive the love and caring attention of these craftspeople have a vital force; a soul. As we are a Japanese car company, we believe that a form sincerely and painstakingly made by human hands receives a soul."

3 For Maeda, design is about much more than just the way each Mazda car looks. He is interested in designing the image for the Mazda brand, so that all the cars share a common theme. The idea is that when customers see all the cars together, they can feel this theme running through each design — that theme is of course KODO.

チーターをモチーフにした魂動デザインのデザインオブジェ

4 What perhaps distinguishes the design team at Mazda from other car makers is the process involved. At Mazda, designers do not begin by drawing new designs for cars. Instead, they create objects with various different forms, and consider how these forms make people feel. They then work from those forms to design new models for their cars.

5 Traditionally, designers would talk with the engineers and reach a

compromise between the ideal style and the practical constraints of making a car. Designers at Mazda are no longer forced to compromise, and their job is to design cars that inspire the engineers to create cars that fulfill the designs. Engineers work hard to turn the vision of the designers into a reality.

店内の様子

6 Mazda design represents the whole of Mazda as a brand, and goes beyond cars, with the design concept even shaping their new type of sales outlets, called New-Generation Showrooms. Under the supervision of Mazda's Design Division, the new showrooms are built using black, white and silver, with wood as accents to create a relaxing space for customers. Everything is designed meticulously to ensure that both the cars on display and the space itself create the perfect atmosphere. This means the number of light bulbs, and even their angles to illuminate the displays inside, are all considered.

新世代店舗の外観

7 So, how have the new showrooms been received by customers? According to the staff working in one such showroom, there has already been a noticeable change in the response of customers. The exterior design of the new showrooms attracts passers-by, who take more of an interest in the cars on display than before. Once inside, both new and repeat customers seem to sense the upgraded brand image of Mazda.

店内の様子

車のメンテナンスサービスを行う整備士

8 However, despite the importance of design, it is the quality of the cars that staff are most keen to emphasize. "We want our customers to feel the joy of driving," one of the mechanics says. A member of the sales staff also adds, "Whatever customers expect in cars; fuel efficiency, functions, or design… our job is to listen to each customer individually, and try to find the best car to suit his or her needs and tastes."

■店舗関連の取材及び画像提供協力：株式会社京滋マツダ長岡京店

> **NOTES**
> ◆ ll. 8-9 **Zoom-Zoom** もともとはクルマの走行音を表す英語の子供言葉。人が子供の時に体験した動くことへの感動を愛し続けられるような商品造りを目指すマツダブランドを表現したもの。　◆ ll. 12-13 **KODO: Soul of Motion** 魂動　◆ l. 14 **Ikuo Maeda** 前田育男　◆ l. 49 **New-Generation Showrooms** 新世代店舗

1 Synonym Questions

以下の語句の同意語を選びましょう。単語の左側の数字はその語句が出てくる本文の段落番号です。

1. 1 aware　　　_____
2. 1 evident　　_____
3. 1 launch　　 _____
4. 2 particularly _____
5. 5 traditionally _____
6. 5 inspire　　_____
7. 6 outlet　　 _____
8. 7 response　 _____
9. 7 attract　　_____
10. 8 individually _____

| clear | especially | separately | stimulate | conscious |
| fascinate | shop | conventionally | reaction | start |

2 Questions & Answers

質問の答えとして正しいものを一つ選びましょう。

1. Who is Ikuo Maeda?

    (A) A staff member who works in a showroom

    (B) The designer who created the Mazda R360

    (C) The former chief of a department at Mazda

2. What is true about 'KODO: Soul of Motion'?

    (A) It is based on the beauty of car movement in particular.

    (B) It was created because Mazda changed its focus.

    (C) It was introduced half a century after the debut of the Mazda R360.

3. What is true about the New-Generation Showrooms?

    (A) Mazda's Design Division leaves the choice of the interior design up to staff there.

    (B) Thanks to the exterior design of the showrooms, people are more attracted to the cars on display.

    (C) They are made almost completely from wood in order to make customers feel relaxed.

Comprehension Check

本文の内容に合うものを一つ選びましょう。

1. 1～2段落に関して
   (A) According to Mr. Maeda, KODO Design represents the dynamic beauty of life.
   (B) Mazda is aware that a fashion item reflects the taste and sense of style of many people.
   (C) Mr. Maeda says that car companies believe cars get a 'soul' from craftspeople.
   (D) The appearance of the Mazda R360 makes us fully understand that Mazda has focused on design from the start.

2. 3～5段落に関して
   (A) Designers at Mazda begin to draw a new car design after considering how people feel toward various forms.
   (B) Designers at Mazda have never made a compromise with engineers in making cars since the company's foundation.
   (C) Mr. Maeda says he only has an interest in the way Mazda cars look.
   (D) The job of designers at Mazda is to design cars, not to inspire engineers.

3. 6～8段落に関して
   (A) As for Mazda's new showrooms, different colors are used in different shops.
   (B) Even the angles of light bulbs are carefully considered so that the perfect atmosphere is created in Mazda's new showrooms.
   (C) Mazda's sales staff put emphasis on the design of the cars, not on their quality.
   (D) Passers-by who are attracted by the exterior design of Mazda's new showrooms seem to get confused once they enter inside.

4 Composition

あなたが興味をもっている企業についてホームページなどで事実を調べ、例文を参考にして以下の空欄にあてはまる語句を入れて、その企業の説明を英語でしてみましょう。参照する企業は、例文ごとに変えても、すべて同じ企業でもかまいません。

例1 Mazda's new concept for the design of their cars is based on the beauty of animal movement.
マツダのカーデザインの新しいコンセプトは、動物の動きの美しさを基にしている。

企業名 _____
(　　　　)'s new concept for (　　　　　) is based on (　　　　　).

例2 What perhaps distinguishes the design team at Mazda from other car makers is the process involved.
マツダのデザインチームが他の自動車メーカーと異なっているのは、関わっている工程である。

企業名 _____
What perhaps distinguishes (　　　　) from (　　　　) is (　　　　).

例3 The exterior design of the new showrooms of Mazda attracts passers-by.
マツダの新ショールームの外観のデザインは、道行く人々を引きつけている。

企業名 _____
(　　　　) of (　　　　) attracts (　　　　).

5 Filling in the Blanks

本文を要約した下記の英文を読み、空欄にあてはまる単語を選択肢から選び、必要に応じて活用させて入れましょう。

> KODO is a design concept that Mazda's Design Division (①　　　) in 2010, representing the company's focus on animal movement. As a Japanese (②　　　), Mazda follows the traditional Japanese way of thinking in which objects that craftspeople make with love and caring attention have a (③　　　). KODO Design is the common theme (④　　　) by all the cars to (⑤　　　) the image of the Mazda brand as a whole. Mazda's Design Division also (⑥　　　) the design of the company's new showrooms including both the interior and exterior. The new showrooms contribute to (⑦　　　) Mazda's brand image, with (⑧　　　) space and effective (⑨　　　) of cars. Staff working there do not forget, however, to try to find the best car for customers, according to their (⑩　　　) needs and tastes.

| display | individual | launch | manufacturer | relaxing |
| represent | share | soul | supervise | upgrading |

マツダ魁　CONCEPT

車の内装について説明する販売店社員

Chapter 6

UCC
UCC 上島珈琲

企業紹介

UCC 上島珈琲は、1933年の創業から85年以上に亘り、コーヒーを核に世界唯一の「カップから農園まで」一貫した事業を構築し、グローバルにその領域を広げてきました。コーヒー専業メーカーとして長年蓄積してきた専門知識・ノウハウのもと、多様なお客様のニーズに対応するおいしいコーヒーづくりに取り組んでいます。2018年7月、1969年に開発した世界初の缶コーヒー「UCCミルクコーヒー」が販売期間49年で缶コーヒーのロングセラー製品としてギネス世界記録®に認定されました。

Grammar Tips for the TOEIC® L&R Test

2つの名詞（のはたらきをするかたまり）をつなぐ**現在分詞**に注意しよう。

本文では以下の表現が見られます。

As the business expanded, UCC began the nationwide rollout of UCC Coffee Bazaar, a specialty store offering roasted beans and custom grinds.

上の例では現在分詞 offering が a specialty store と roasted beans and custom grinds という 2 つの名詞のかたまりをつないでいます。

例題を見てみましょう。

> The project has already accomplished results (　　) initial expectations.
> (A) exceed
> (B) exceeded
> (C) exceeding
> (D) exceedingly

文の述語動詞は has accomplished なので (A) や (B) の動詞は入らないし、(D) の副詞を入れると空欄の直後の名詞のかたまり initial expectations が文の中で浮いてしまいます。したがって、results と initial expectations という 2 つの名詞のかたまりをつなぐ語を選択することになるわけですが、exceed は第 4 文型も第 5 文型もとらない動詞なので、(B) の過去分詞 exceeded でつなぐことはできません。2 つの名詞をつなぐことができるのは、results that exceeded initial expectations の意味を表す (C) の現在分詞 exceeding です。

Vocabulary Questions

以下の語句の意味を、下の語群から選びましょう。

1. allow _____
2. amazed _____
3. beverage _____
4. complete _____
5. decade _____
6. eventually _____
7. founder _____
8. gradually _____
9. major _____
10. meet _____
11. notice _____
12. offer _____
13. organization _____
14. protect _____
15. receive _____
16. set up _____
17. social _____
18. succeed _____
19. variety _____
20. well-known _____

種類	社交の	徐々に	〜を受け取る
団体	主要な	成功する	〜を設置する
飲み物	有名な	〜に気づく	〜を提供する
十年間	びっくりした	〜を満たす	〜を保護する
創設者	ついに	〜を認める	〜を完成させる

Language in Use

 Audio 1-12

音声を聴いて空欄を埋めましょう。さらに、完成した文の日本語訳を下線部に書きましょう。

1. The regional sales manager felt confident that (　　　)(　　　)(　　　)(　　　).

   _____

2. Japanese compact cars (　　　)(　　　)(　　　)(　　　) overseas markets.

   _____

3. The notable chef (　　　)(　　　)(　　　)(　　　) the food into Japan.

   _____

Reading

1 Some people say that the history of coffee drinking goes back over 1,000 years. According to a legend, an Ethiopian goat farmer noticed that his goats seemed more active after eating coffee berries. He told a local monk, who then tried a drink made out of the berries. Because of that drink, he could stay awake all night. Since then, coffee has become one of the world's most popular drinks, with many varieties and ways of drinking it.

2 It is widely believed that coffee first arrived in Japan through Dutch and Portuguese merchants in the 1700s. Coffee gradually became known in the Rokumeikan era (1883-1887). In 1888, the very first café in Japan, Kahisakan, opened in Tokyo. At that time, cafés were a social place for upper-class people, scholars, and literary writers. From the 1920s, coffee gradually became popular among the general public. Then after World War II, as people started eating western food more often, coffee's consumption increased. However, there was one person instrumental in this popularization, Tadao Ueshima, the founder of the well-known coffee company, UCC.

3 In 1933, Ueshima founded a company, Ueshima Tadao Shoten, dealing in imported food products such as butter and jam. A few years later, Ueshima first tried coffee in Kobe. He was amazed at the taste, beginning his lifelong fascination with the drink, and eventually he decided to start a coffee business. Things went well until the beginning of World War II, when the importation of coffee was banned by the government.

4 After the war was over, Ueshima was ready to start importing coffee again. In 1950, when imports were allowed again, UCC started to import coffee from Colombia. The following year, Ueshima Coffee Co., Ltd. was established.

5 One of UCC's major innovations was its canned coffee. One day, while traveling around Japan on business, Ueshima bought a bottle of milk coffee to drink. He hadn't finished it when his train was about to leave, so he had to return his unfinished drink to the store. He couldn't forget this, and eventually he struck upon the idea of coffee in a can. If coffee was in a can, he could take it with him on the train! It could be kept and sold at normal temperature as well. It took a long time to perfect a way of keeping the taste of the coffee fresh in the can but eventually UCC

succeeded, and the first canned coffee beverage was released in 1969. After it was introduced at Expo 1970 in Osaka, canned coffee went on to become one of the most popular ways to drink coffee in Japan.

6 In the same year, the construction of UCC's Osaka factory was completed. It was the first fully automated coffee factory in Japan. It was also the first in Japan to manufacture vacuum-packed coffee. This eventually contributed to the industrialization of coffee manufacturing in Japan. As the business

expanded, UCC began the nationwide rollout of UCC Coffee Bazaar, a specialty store offering roasted beans and custom grinds. The company also provided ways to enjoy coffee at home with home-use coffee products, and these quickly became popular.

7 UCC was also one of the first companies in the world to establish their own coffee estate. The establishment of UCC's coffee estate in Jamaica in 1981 meant that UCC secured a stable way to access top quality "Blue Mountain" coffee beans. It also became the first Caribbean coffee estate to receive the "Rainforest Alliance" certification in 2008. This certification is awarded to organizations which meet ethical standards for

protecting the environment, as well as the farmers working on the estates. In 1989, UCC opened another coffee estate on the Big Island in Hawaii, producing the local "Kona" coffee beans.

8 Over the last few decades, UCC has made inroads into many markets outside Japan. Beginning with the establishment of offices in Brazil and Singapore in 1984, the company has since set up offices in over 20 countries around the world, including Asia and Europe. Due to his major influence on Japan's coffee culture, the International Coffee Organization bestowed a monument in 1988, referring to Ueshima as "the father of coffee in Japan," and now UCC has become synonymous with high quality coffee around the world.

NOTES

◆ l. 10 Rokumeikan　鹿鳴館　◆ l. 11 Kahisakan　可否茶館　◆ l. 20 Ueshima Tadao Shoten　上島忠雄商店　◆ l. 28 Ueshima Coffee Co., Ltd.　上島珈琲株式会社　◆ l. 50 UCC Coffee Bazaar　UCCコーヒーバザール　◆ l. 59 "Rainforest Alliance" certification　レインフォレスト・アライアンス認証　◆ ll. 69-70 the International Coffee Organization　国際コーヒー機関

1 Synonym Questions

以下の語句の同意語を選びましょう。単語の左側の数字はその語句が出てくる本文の段落番号です。

1. **1** notice _____
2. **1** active _____
3. **2** gradually _____
4. **2** instrumental _____
5. **2** well-known _____
6. **3** ban _____
7. **6** fully _____
8. **7** stable _____
9. **7** meet _____
10. **8** bestow _____

| entirely | helpful | observe | slowly | firm |
| lively | prohibit | grant | noted | satisfy |

2 Questions & Answers

質問の答えとして正しいものを一つ選びましょう。

1. What is true about the history of coffee?

    (A) All classes of society drank it at the opening of Kahisakan.

    (B) An Ethiopian goat farmer was the first to drink it.

    (C) It first arrived in Japan in the 18th century.

2. What is true about Tadao Ueshima?

    (A) He became charmed by the flavor of coffee on his first try.

    (B) He called himself "the father of coffee in Japan."

    (C) He struck upon the idea of canned coffee on a train platform.

3. Where is one of UCC's coffee estates?

    (A) In Africa

    (B) In Brazil

    (C) In the U.S.

3 Comprehension Check

本文の内容に合うものを一つ選びましょう。

1. ①〜③段落に関して
   (A) Legend has it that the first person to try coffee spent a whole night wide-awake.
   (B) Tadao's business proceeded smoothly even after the government prohibited the importation of coffee.
   (C) There are many kinds of coffee, but there are limited ways of drinking it.
   (D) Though Western food became more popular after the war, coffee's popularity remained unchanged.

2. ④〜⑥段落に関して
   (A) Tadao changed his company's name to Ueshima Coffee Co., Ltd. in order to start importing coffee again.
   (B) UCC developed a way of keeping the flavor of canned coffee fresh in a short period of time.
   (C) UCC's canned coffee was successful at Expo 1970 in Osaka, but its popularity didn't last long.
   (D) UCC's production of vacuum-packed coffee led to the eventual industrialization of coffee manufacturing in Japan.

3. ⑦〜⑧段落に関して
   (A) "Rainforest Alliance" certification is awarded to organizations when they meet the sales standards of a product.
   (B) The establishment of UCC's office in Singapore follows that of its second coffee estate in Hawaii.
   (C) UCC gave the International Coffee Organization a monument because it strongly influenced Japan's coffee culture.
   (D) UCC's management of its coffee estate in Jamaica meant that it could get "Blue Mountain" coffee beans steadily.

4 Composition

あなたが興味をもっている企業についてホームページなどで事実を調べ、例文を参考にして以下の空欄にあてはまる語句を入れて、その企業の説明を英語でしてみましょう。参照する企業は、例文ごとに変えても、すべて同じ企業でもかまいません。

例1 In 1950, UCC started to import coffee from Colombia.
1950年に、UCCはコロンビアからのコーヒーの輸入を開始した。

企業名 _____
In (   ), (   ) started to import (   ) from (   ).

例2 One of UCC's major innovations was its canned coffee.
UCCの画期的な開発商品のひとつは缶コーヒーだった。

企業名 _____
One of (   )'s major innovations was its (   ).

例3 In 1970, the construction of UCC's Osaka factory was completed.
1970年に、UCCの大阪工場の建設が完了した。

企業名 _____
In (   ), the construction of (   )'s (   ) was completed.

Chapter 6

5 Chronological Table

本文の内容に基づいて、以下の年表を完成させましょう。

年　号	出　来　事
（①　　　）頃	オランダとポルトガルの商人によりコーヒーが日本にもたらされる。
（②　　　）	上島忠雄が（③　　　　　）を扱う上島忠雄商店を創業する。
その数年後	上島がコーヒー事業を始める決意をする。
（④　　　）	政府により大戦開始後禁止されていたコーヒーの輸入を再開する。
1951 年	（⑤　　　　　）が設立される。
（⑥　　　）	世界初の（⑦　　　　　）飲料が発売される。
1970 年	（⑦　　　　）が（⑧　　　　　）で紹介され、広く普及する。
（⑨　　　）	日本初のフルオートメーションコーヒー工場である大阪工場が完成する。
1981 年	自社（⑩　　　　）をジャマイカに、その後ハワイ島にも開設する。
（⑪　　　）	ブラジルとシンガポールに事業所を開設する。
1988 年	国際コーヒー機関が上島を（⑫　　　　　）としてモニュメントを授ける。
現在	世界 20 か国以上で事業を展開し、世界中で UCC は高品質コーヒーの代名詞となっている。

1969 年 4 月　　1978 年　　1981 年　　1986 年

ミルクコーヒーの歴史

2010 年

現在の
ミルクコーヒー

1994 年　　2000 年　　2001 年　　2003 年

Chapter 7

Daifuku
ダイフク

企業紹介
1937年に大阪市西淀川区で創業したダイフクは、モノを動かす技術（マテリアルハンドリング）の総合メーカーです。自動化・省力化が求められる生産・流通・サービスの様々な分野における現場で、保管、搬送、仕分け・ピッキング、情報システムという多様な要素を組み合わせ、市場ごとに特化した最適・最良のシステム・機器を開発してきました。現在、世界23の国と地域の拠点で事業を展開しており、海外従業員数、海外売上ともに高比率を誇るグローバル企業です。

Grammar Tips for the TOEIC® L&R Test

文の主語になれるのは名詞（のはたらきをするかたまり）だけです。

本文では以下の表現が見られます。

With big advances in IT technology in the 2000s, **demand** for semiconductors, which act as the computer brain, along with flat-panel displays used in computer monitors and flat screen TVs, **increased**.

長い一文ですが、文の述語動詞は最後の単語 increased であり、その主語は名詞 demand です。

例題を見てみましょう。

> (　　) of the region's natural resources has been proceeding rapidly.
> (A) Developed
> (B) Developer
> (C) Developing
> (D) Development

ここでは、resources は前置詞 of の目的語であり文の主語ではありませんので、空欄にはこの文の主語が入ることになります。文の主語になることができるのは名詞（のはたらきをするかたまり）だけですから、(B)・(C)・(D) に正答の可能性がありますが、(B) Developer の前にはやはり冠詞が必要ですし、動名詞としての (C) Developing を入れるならば、空欄の直後の前置詞が不要です。したがって、ここでは (D) Development が正答となります。

Vocabulary Questions

以下の語句の意味を、下の語群から選びましょう。

1. advance _____
2. baggage claim _____
3. branch _____
4. deliver _____
5. demand _____
6. increasingly _____
7. luggage _____
8. operate _____
9. passenger _____
10. pharmacy _____
11. pick up _____
12. primarily _____
13. region _____
14. replace _____
15. restoration _____
16. retailer _____
17. sort _____
18. store _____
19. warehouse _____
20. weigh _____

支店	倉庫	手荷物受取所	〜を配達する
修復	地域	主に	〜を保管する
需要	薬局	ますます	〜を取りに行く
乗客	小売業者	営業する	〜を取り替える
進歩	手荷物類	〜を仕分ける	〜の重さをはかる

Language in Use

🔊 Audio 1-14

音声を聴いて空欄を埋めましょう。さらに、完成した文の日本語訳を下線部に書きましょう。

1. These goods ( )( )( )( )( ) among office workers.

   _____

2. Nancy ( )( )( )( )( ) the office-automation equipment.

   _____

3. ( )( )( )( )( ) that he will be promoted to factory manager.

   _____

Reading

🔊 Audio 1-15 **DAIFUKU**

1️⃣ Day-to-day life is becoming ever more convenient. With a few taps on a smartphone we can buy almost any product we want online at any time, and have the order delivered the very next day.

2️⃣ How is this possible?

3️⃣ Traditionally, a shopping experience involved going directly to a store, buying the product we want, and taking it home. If the desired product was not sold at that specific store, we had to find one that did. Now, it is different. Without the need for wholesalers and retailers, companies can directly link to consumers to meet their demands. Daifuku is a company that provides material handling systems such as storage, transport, and sorting and picking systems. These are increasingly important as part of the social infrastructure essential in such a logistics revolution.

4️⃣ In 1937, Daifuku was established as Sakaguchi Kikai Seisakusho Ltd. in Nishiyodogawa-ku, Osaka. The company primarily manufactured cranes and forge rolling machinery for ironworks. After World War II, as Japan entered its period of rapid economic growth, the company moved to manufacture chain conveyor systems, the leading edge of automation systems at the time. Afterwards, Daifuku expanded overseas to support the global expansion of Japanese manufacturers, notably within the automobile industry. Daifuku currently has affiliate companies and offices operating in 23 countries and regions.

5️⃣ Since the 1990s, Daifuku has been active in product development in the distribution sector. Developed in 1966, Daifuku's automated storage and retrieval system, which is essential in manufacturing and distribution systems, has been in demand globally. As the needs for material handling systems have increased, Daifuku has continued to develop new products for storage, transport, sorting and picking.

6️⃣ Daifuku is also prominent in the cleanroom industry. With big advances in IT technology in the 2000s, demand for semiconductors, which act as the computer brain, along with flat-panel displays used in computer monitors and flat screen TVs, increased. Daifuku supplies transport and storage systems for the components used in manufacturing semiconductors and flat-panel displays.

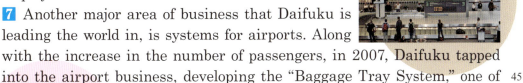

7 Another major area of business that Daifuku is leading the world in, is systems for airports. Along with the increase in the number of passengers, in 2007, Daifuku tapped into the airport business, developing the "Baggage Tray System," one of the fastest baggage handling / transport systems in the world. Using RFID tags and special trays, the system can transport bags at a speed of 600 meters per minute, without losing or damaging the baggage.

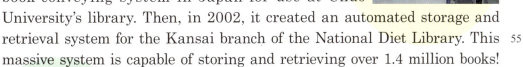

8 The systems that Daifuku has developed over the years are not only business-orientated. In 1978, the company developed the first book-conveying system in Japan for use at Chuo University's library. Then, in 2002, it created an automated storage and retrieval system for the Kansai branch of the National Diet Library. This massive system is capable of storing and retrieving over 1.4 million books! When it was installed, it was the largest book storage and retrieval system in Japan.

9 Daifuku's systems have also aided Japan's historic buildings. In 1980, its trolley conveyor was used for the restoration of the "Hall of the Great Buddha" at Todaiji Temple in Nara. At that time, the hall was the largest wooden building in the world — the same height as a 15-story building. Repair work on the roof was notably dangerous and difficult, with 56,900 roof tiles, each one weighing about 15 kg, needing to be replaced. Daifuku's chain conveyer was extremely helpful in improving work efficiency and safety. The project took place over 10 months and saw no accidents.

10 The systems that Daifuku designs contribute to society by supporting social structures behind the scenes in Japan and the world. The next time you receive items ordered on the internet, collect your luggage from a baggage claim area in an airport, pick up medicine from the pharmacy, or even take out a book from the library, there is a high chance that Daifuku was involved at some stage of the process!

> **NOTES**
> ◆ l. 12 **material handling** マテリアル・ハンドリング ◆ ll. 13-14 **storage, transport, and sorting and picking** 保管、搬送、仕分け・ピッキング
> ◆ l. 17 **Sakaguchi Kikai Seisakusho Ltd.** 株式会社坂口機械製作所 ◆ ll. 28-29 **automated storage and retrieval system** 自動保管出入庫システム ◆ ll. 46-47 **RFID tags** RFID（radio frequency identification）とは、近距離無線通信による自動認識技術を指す。ICタグを使い、様々なモノを識別・管理する。 ◆ l. 55 **the Kansai branch of the National Diet Library** 国会図書館関西館

1 Synonym Questions

以下の語句の同意語を選びましょう。単語の左側の数字はその語句が出てくる本文の段落番号です。

1. 3 involve _____
2. 4 primarily _____
3. 4 rapid _____
4. 4 afterwards _____
5. 4 notably _____
6. 5 essential _____
7. 9 aid _____
8. 9 restoration _____
9. 9 notably _____
10. 10 chance _____

| assist | particularly | remarkably | subsequently | chiefly |
| possibility | repair | indispensable | quick | require |

2 Questions & Answers

質問の答えとして正しいものを一つ選びましょう。

1. What did Daifuku begin to develop some time after the war?
    (A) Automated warehouse systems
    (B) Chain conveyor systems
    (C) Forge rolling machinery

2. What does Daifuku provide for the cleanroom industry?
    (A) Automated warehouse systems
    (B) Baggage handling / transport systems
    (C) Transport and storage systems

3. What was installed in the Kansai branch of the National Diet Library?
    (A) A manufacturing and distribution system
    (B) A transport and storage system
    (C) An automated storage and retrieval system

3 Comprehension Check

本文の内容に合うものを一つ選びましょう。

1. ①〜④段落に関して
   (A) Daifuku was greatly interested in material handling systems since its foundation.
   (B) In more recent ways of shopping, we have to go around to several stores until we find what we want.
   (C) It is hard to get something we purchase online by overnight delivery.
   (D) When Daifuku found its way into making chain conveyor systems, they were the most advanced automation systems.

2. ⑤〜⑦段落に関して
   (A) Daifuku had expanded into the airport business before it became busy developing products in the distribution sector.
   (B) Daifuku is prominent in manufacturing semiconductors and flat-panel displays in the cleanroom industry.
   (C) Daifuku's automated storage and retrieval system, developed more than 50 years ago, has been in demand all over the world.
   (D) The "Baggage Tray System" conveys bags at low speeds so that they won't be damaged or lost.

3. ⑧〜⑩段落に関して
   (A) Daifuku's "behind the scenes" products support social structures all over the world.
   (B) Due to Daifuku's chain conveyer, repair work at Todaiji was completed in ten months without any trouble.
   (C) Restoration work at Todaiji was highly dangerous and difficult because so many light roof tiles which were in high places needed replacing.
   (D) The largest book storage and retrieval system in Japan was installed at Chuo University's library in 1978.

4 Composition

あなたが興味をもっている企業についてホームページなどで事実を調べ、例文を参考にして以下の空欄にあてはまる語句を入れて、その企業の説明を英語でしてみましょう。参照する企業は、例文ごとに変えても、すべて同じ企業でもかまいません。

例 1 In <u>1937</u>, <u>Daifuku</u> was established as <u>Sakaguchi Kikai Seisakusho Ltd.</u> in <u>Nishiyodogawa-ku, Osaka</u>.

1937 年にダイフクは株式会社坂口機械製作所として大阪市西淀川区に設立された。

企業名 _____

In (　　　　), (　　　　　　) was established as (　　　　　　) in (　　　　　　).

例 2 <u>Daifuku</u> currently has <u>affiliate companies and offices</u> operating in <u>23 countries and regions</u>.

ダイフクには現在 23 の国と地域で営業するグループ会社と事務所がある。

企業名 _____

(　　　　　　) currently has (　　　　　　) operating in (　　　　　　).

例 3 Since <u>the 1990's</u>, <u>Daifuku</u> has been active in <u>product development</u> in the <u>distribution</u> sector.

1990 年代から、ダイフクは物流分野における製品開発に積極的に取り組んでいる。

企業名 _____

Since (　　　　　　), (　　　　　　) has been active in (　　　　　　) in the (　　　　　　) sector.

5 Chronological Table

本文の内容に基づいて、以下の年表を完成させましょう。

年　号	出　来　事
（①　　　　）	大阪市西淀川区に株式会社坂口機械製作所として設立され、クレーンや製鉄用の鍛圧機を製造する。
戦後	オートメーションシステムの最先端であった（②　　　　　　）システムの製造へと移行する。
1966年	（③　　　　　　）システムを開発する。
（④　　　　）	中央大学図書館に、日本初の書籍搬送システムを設置する。
1980年	（⑤　　　　　　）の修復作業で（⑥　　　　　　）が使用される。
1990年代以来	（⑦　　　　　　）部門の製品開発を積極的におこなっている。
（⑧　　　　）	自動倉庫システムを開発し、（⑨　　　　　　）に設置する。
（⑩　　　　）	空港事業に参入し、その後、（⑪　　　　　　）を開発する。
現在	日本国内だけでなく、世界の（⑫　　　　　　）の国と地域にあるグループ会社と事業所でさまざまな事業をおこなっている。

ロゴの変遷

1947年に「大福機工株式会社」に社名変更、ロゴを制定

1984年に社名を「株式会社ダイフク」に変更

1969年に漢字からカタカナロゴへ

1998年に日本のダイフクから世界のDAIFUKUへ

Chapter 8

Sakura Color Products
サクラクレパス

企業紹介

サクラクレパスは、大阪・森ノ宮に本社を置く総合文具メーカーです。1921年に創業し、「櫻クレィヨン」の製造と販売を開始しました。最高品質の商品を提供することで教育・文化に貢献し、国の繁栄とともに歩むため、国花である"さくら"の名称とマークを製品に冠しました。1925年には、世界で初めて「クレパス」を開発。その後、「クーピー」や筆記具などの商品も生まれました。現在では、100カ国を越える国で展開しています。

Grammar Tips for the TOEIC® L&R Test

主語と動詞の単数・複数の一致を押さえておこう。

本文では以下の表現が見られます。

The colorful tin packaging for the pencils has remained unchanged since their introduction.

上の例では、文の主語は、動詞 has remained の直前の pencils ではなく、packaging ですから、動詞は単数形でよいわけです。

例題を見てみましょう。

> Today's topic at the workshop for young actors (　) me a lot.
> (A) interest
> (B) interesting
> (C) interestingly
> (D) interests

まず、(B) や (C) を選ぶとこの文から述語動詞がなくなってしまい、文として成立しなくなるので、動詞である (A) か (D) から選びます。そして、この文の主語は、空欄の直前の複数形の名詞 actors ではなく、もっと前にある単数形の名詞 topic ですから、(A) を選択しないように注意が必要です。

以前にくらべると出題数は減りましたが、このパターンは確実に出題されます。TOEIC® L&R では Part 5 をできるだけ短い時間で通過することがスコアアップのポイントですが、あわてて解答して「ひっかけ」に引っかかってしまわないように注意をしましょう。

Vocabulary Questions

以下の語句の意味を、下の語群から選びましょう。

1. accomplish　_____
2. affect　_____
3. beneficial　_____
4. combine　_____
5. conventional　_____
6. existing　_____
7. face　_____
8. improve　_____
9. increase　_____
10. ingredient　_____
11. invention　_____
12. opportunity　_____
13. ordinary　_____
14. presence　_____
15. quality　_____
16. resolve　_____
17. revolutionary　_____
18. stationery　_____
19. submission　_____
20. visible　_____

機会	存在感	画期的な	～を改善する
材料	有益な	目に見える	～に直面する
提出	従来の	現存している	～を成し遂げる
発明	良質の	～を増やす	～を組み合わせる
文房具	ふつうの	～を解決する	～に影響を与える

Language in Use

 Audio 1-16

音声を聴いて空欄を埋めましょう。さらに、完成した文の日本語訳を下線部に書きましょう。

1. The arguments from the politician (　　　)(　　　)(　　　) the voters.

   _____

2. The new CEO firstly (　　　)(　　　)(　　　) the company's debt to its main bank.

   _____

3. The enterprise will (　　　)(　　　)(　　　) in the hospitality industry.

   _____

Reading

1 What is art and how should you teach it? Should students be encouraged to make perfect copies of an existing picture, or given creative freedom to express themselves in any way they like? Kanae Yamamoto was a Japanese artist who traveled to Europe in the Taisho period. After he came back to Japan, he promoted freedom in art, particularly in children's education, which he called "Jiyu-ga." He believed that drawing would increase children's creativity, and that vivid colors would also be beneficial.

2 In those days, copying models was the way Japanese children were taught to draw. They had little opportunity to express themselves with art. Yamamoto's ideas were revolutionary at that time, and hit home with Rinzo Satake and Shokoh Sasaki. They decided to create a high quality crayon that would facilitate art and increase creativity. To accomplish this goal, in 1921 the Japan Crayon Company, known today as Sakura Color Products, was founded.

3 From the start, the company worked hard to develop a quality crayon, and in 1925 invented the first-ever Cray-Pas, combining both oil and pigment. The name Cray-Pas derives from the words crayon and pastel. Cray-Pas contained coconut oil and another oil as the base, but at first these oils were affected by extreme temperatures of summer and winter in Japan. However, in 1928 it was improved so that it could be used in any season. This formula is basically unchanged and still in use today.

4 The passion to encourage artistic creativity in children and adults can be seen throughout the history of Sakura. At the end of World War II, Japan was a devastated country, with seemingly little hope for the future. Many children faced suffering, and Sakura decided to sponsor Cray-Pas Train Sketch Tours. In total the company sponsored more than ten tours in Tokyo and other parts of Japan, encouraging children to draw and to be positive in order to raise their hopes for the future.

5 As famous as the Cray-Pas is the Coupy Pencil, first launched in 1973. It was designed to resolve three common problems with color pencils. The

lead of color pencils breaks easily; it is hard to color over a wide area; and you can't rub out what you wrote with a normal eraser. Coupy pencils got rid of the wood around the pencil, and made the lead thicker, in fact, twice as thick as an ordinary color pencil. This means that the pencil does not break, and can color over a wide area. Also, because the pencil is made from special ingredients, any coloring can be easily erased. The colorful tin packaging for the pencils has remained unchanged since their introduction, so that it reminds some people of their childhood. The pencils are so well-known that they have almost become a part of Japanese culture.

6 Although Sakura will always have a place in history for the invention of their Cray-Pas and then Coupy Pencil, the company has continued to create new products. In 1984, Sakura launched "Ballsign," the world's first water-based gel ink ballpoint pen. The inks in these pens are more clearly visible than conventional ones. Now most stationery companies produce gel-based ink pens, and they are very popular with comic book artists.

7 Based in Osaka, the company now has a worldwide presence, with the establishment of Sakura Color Products of America, Inc. in California in 1986, and Shanghai Sakura International Trading Co., Ltd. in Shanghai in 2002. Following the company tradition of contributing to education and culture, in 1995 Sakura of America started a national art competition for children in America. It is for students from kindergarten to junior high school, designed to encourage their creativity. The competition is called the Cray-Pas Wonderful Colorful World Contest, and receives around 17,000 submissions every year.

NOTES

◆ l. 3 **Kanae Yamamoto** 山本鼎　◆ l. 6 **Jiyu-ga** 自由画
◆ ll. 12-13 **Rinzo Satake** 佐武林蔵　◆ l. 13 **Shokoh Sasaki** 佐々木昌興　◆ l. 16 **the Japan Crayon Company** 日本クレィヨン商会　◆ l. 63 **Sakura Color Products of America, Inc.** サクラ・カラー・プロダクツ・オブ・アメリカ　◆ l. 64 **Shanghai Sakura International Trading Co., Ltd.** 櫻華国際貿易（上海）有限公司

1 Synonym Questions

以下の語句の同意語を選びましょう。単語の左側の数字はその語句が出てくる本文の段落番号です。

1. **1** freedom _____
2. **1** beneficial _____
3. **2** opportunity _____
4. **2** revolutionary _____
5. **2** accomplish _____
6. **4** passion _____
7. **4** suffering _____
8. **5** ordinary _____
9. **5** erase _____
10. **7** competition _____

| achieve | delete | helpful | unconventional | chance |
| enthusiasm | normal | contest | hardship | liberty |

2 Questions & Answers

質問の答えとして正しいものを一つ選びましょう。

1. Who was Kanae Yamamoto?

    (A) A man who wanted to give children freedom in art

    (B) An artist who encouraged children to copy models

    (C) One of the founders of the Japan Crayon Company

2. Why did Cray-Pas need to be improved after its introduction in 1925?

    (A) To add coconut oil to it

    (B) To make a combination of oil and pigment

    (C) To make it fit for Japanese weather

3. What is true about the contest conducted by Sakura of America?

    (A) It was started in order to make cultural and educational contributions.

    (B) More than 20 thousand artworks are submitted every year.

    (C) Preschool children can't participate in it.

3 Comprehension Check

本文の内容に合うものを一つ選びましょう。

1. ①〜②段落に関して
   (A) Children were lucky enough to express themselves with art in the Taisho period.
   (B) "Jiyu-ga" teaches students to make an exact copy of the original.
   (C) Yamamoto thought it beneficial for children to draw without bright colors.
   (D) Yamamoto's way of thinking about art strongly impacted the ideas of Satake and Sasaki.

2. ③〜④段落に関して
   (A) The formula for Cray-Pas has changed completely since its invention.
   (B) The improved Cray-Pas launched in 1928 was used for the limited period of one year.
   (C) The name Cray-Pas originates from the ingredients of crayon and pastel.
   (D) The tours Sakura sponsored were for the purpose of giving children hope for the future.

3. ⑤〜⑦段落に関して
   (A) Any coloring with the Coupy Pencil can be easily deleted with a special eraser.
   (B) Comic book artists enjoy using Ballsign rather than other makers' gel-based ink pens.
   (C) Sakura established companies in the U.S. and China just before and after the start of the 20th century, respectively.
   (D) The container for the Coupy Pencil has stayed the same since it was introduced.

4 Composition

あなたが興味をもっている企業についてホームページなどで事実を調べ、例文を参考にして以下の空欄にあてはまる語句を入れて、その企業の説明を英語でしてみましょう。参照する企業は、例文ごとに変えても、すべて同じ企業でもかまいません。

例1 The name Cray-Pas derives from the words crayon and pastel.
クレパスという名前はクレヨンとパステルという言葉に由来する。

企業名 _____
The name ( ) derives from ( ).

例2 As famous as the Cray-Pas is the Coupy Pencil, first launched in 1973.
クレパスと同じく有名なものはクーピーペンシルで、1973年に発売された。

企業名 _____
As famous as ( ) is ( ), first launched in ( ).

例3 Sakura of America started a national art competition for children in America.
サクラ・オブ・アメリカはアメリカで子供向けの全国芸術コンクールを始めた。

企業名 _____
( ) started ( ) competition for ( ) in ( ).

5 Chronological Table

本文の内容に基づいて、以下の年表を完成させましょう。

年　号	出　来　事
（①　　）	「自由画運動」を提唱した（②　　　　　）の考えに影響を受けた佐武林蔵と佐々木昌興が（③　　　　　）を創立する。
1925年	（④　　　　　）と（⑤　　　　　）の長所を兼ね備えた（⑥　　　　　）の開発に成功し、販売を始める。
（⑦　　）	（⑥　　　　　）の四季一定品の開発に成功し、販売を始める。
1973年	色鉛筆の短所を解決した（⑧　　　　　）を発売する。
（⑨　　）	世界初の水性ゲルインキボールペンである（⑩　　　　　）を発売する。
（⑪　　）	サクラ・カラー・プロダクツ・オブ・アメリカを設立する。
（⑫　　）	櫻華国際貿易（上海）有限公司を設立する。
現在	ひとびとの未来に貢献すべく、文房具のみならず、さまざまな分野の商品を製造している。

櫻クレィヨン（青箱）

櫻クレィヨン（赤箱）

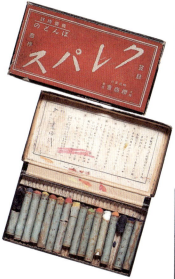

ほんとのクレパス内箱・外箱

現在のクレパス

クーピーペンシル30　カラーオンカラー

Chapter 9

Yanmar
ヤンマー

企業紹介

1912 年に大阪で創業したヤンマーは、1933 年に世界で初めてディーゼルエンジンの小型実用化に成功しました。以来、産業用ディーゼルエンジンを事業の柱とし、さまざまな市場へ商品・サービス・ノウハウを融合したトータルソリューションを提供する総合産業機械メーカーです。小型エンジン、大型エンジン、農業機械・農業施設、建設機械、エネルギーシステム、マリン、工作機械・コンポーネントの 7 事業を有し、グローバルにビジネスを展開しています。

Grammar Tips for the TOEIC® L&R Test

動詞と前置詞のあいだに割り込む副詞に注意しよう。

本文では以下の表現が見られます。

For over a century, Yanmar has contributed greatly to Japan's industry and its people.

上の例では、「～に貢献している」という表現 contribute to の動詞と前置詞のあいだに副詞 greatly が割り込むように入っています。副詞は、いわゆる 5 文型において、名詞や形容詞が入ることができる場所には基本的に入ることができない修飾語だったわけですが、修飾語でしかないからこそ、逆に名詞や形容詞が入っていけない場所に入っていくことができるわけです。

例題を見てみましょう。

> One of the board of directors objected (　　) to the merger with a competitor.
> 　(A) strength
> 　(B) strengthen
> 　(C) strong
> 　(D) strongly

ここでは、object の意味がわからなければ、この語が他動詞（他動詞用法はありますが、that 節を続ける用法しかありません）に見えて、(A) の名詞を選んでしまいがちです。しかし、object to で「～に反対する」意味だと知っていれば、動詞と前置詞のあいだに割り込む副詞 (D) strongly を選択できます。object to は TOEIC® L&R 頻出表現なので覚えておきましょう。

Vocabulary Questions

以下の語句の意味を、下の語群から選びましょう。

1. annually _____
2. carry out _____
3. construction site _____
4. durable _____
5. economy _____
6. environment _____
7. equipment _____
8. essential _____
9. experience _____
10. fuel _____
11. grain _____
12. inventor _____
13. maintain _____
14. material _____
15. operate _____
16. personnel _____
17. previously _____
18. release _____
19. rely on _____
20. technician _____

環境	燃料	耐久性のある	～を経験する
機器	技術者	必要不可欠な	～を実行する
経済	発明者	毎年	～を操作する
穀物	建設現場	以前に	～を発売する
材料	スタッフ	～に頼る	～を維持管理する

Language in Use

 Audio 2-01

音声を聴いて空欄を埋めましょう。さらに、完成した文の日本語訳を下線部に書きましょう。

1. The modern ( )( )( )( )( ) mountains.

   _____

2. Rachel ( )( )( )( )( ) winning the contract for the firm.

   _____

3. The items we deal in ( )( )( )( )( ) clothing.

   _____

Reading

 Audio 2-02

1 Diesel is a kind of fuel that is used in cars, trucks and other forms of transportation. The word comes from the name of the inventor of the diesel engine, Dr. Rudolf Diesel. The invention of diesel engines at the end of the 19th century was very important for industry around the world. It provided a more efficient way of creating energy than the steam engines that were popular at the time. However, the first diesel engines were also very large, had to operate at low speeds, and were hard to handle. A few decades later, the world's first small diesel engine was developed by Magokichi Yamaoka, the founder of Yanmar Corporation. Since then, these small but durable engines have powered everything from farm machinery, to boats, to construction equipment.

2 As is still the case today, the food industry in early 20th century Japan relied heavily on fishing boats and farm machinery. Many of these machines were run on gasoline. However, because Japan is a country surrounded by the sea, this fuel had to be imported by ship, making it an expensive commodity. This reliance on fuel for gasoline engines drove up the cost of food. In 1933, Yanmar introduced a small diesel engine that provided a more efficient way of producing power. It meant that food could be produced more economically and fishing boats could run at lower costs, helping to keep food prices down. The small diesel engine was a hit, and Yanmar grew because of it.

3 Yanmar experienced some setbacks when its factories were damaged in the bombing raids of World War II. Following the war however, Yanmar came back even stronger than before. Yanmar's technology played a big role in rebuilding Japan's economy and industry. In the 1960s, the "combine harvester" and the "rice transplanter," together with the tractor, became essential for many rice farmers. At that time however, combine harvesters were powered with gasoline. In 1969, Yanmar introduced the TC500 walk-behind two-row combine that was powered by diesel. After that, diesel engines became the standard for such machines. In 1972,

Yanmar introduced the "TC750 riding two-row reaper" that could thresh rice without damaging the grains. Innovations such as the TC500 and TC750 made the company well-known around the world.

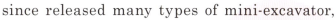

4 During Japan's rapid economic growth in the second half of the 20th century, Yanmar also diversified into construction equipment. The company focused on compact construction equipment, and fitted diesel engines to machines such as the YNB300 wheeled mini-excavator in 1968 and later, the YFW500 rubber-tracked carrier which was used to transport construction materials over soft or uneven ground. The mini-excavator helped to improve efficiency at many small-scale construction sites, where previously earth excavation had been carried out manually. Yanmar has since released many types of mini-excavator, including the very popular YB1200 mini-excavator, first made available in 1975.

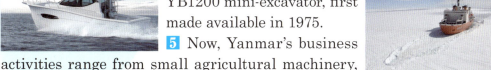

5 Now, Yanmar's business activities range from small agricultural machinery, to marine engines, to construction equipment, and even extremely large engines used at the South Pole! Since 1983, Yanmar's engines have been used to power the Showa Station in Antarctica. In such a cold environment, it is vital that lighting, heating and hot water systems are reliable and remain working at all times. The scientists and personnel who are stationed there depend on them. Yanmar's technicians have been dispatched to the National Institute of Polar Research annually. There, as members of the Japan Antarctic Research Expedition Team, they contribute to maintaining power generators under harsh conditions, protecting the power of Showa Station.

6 For over a century, Yanmar has contributed greatly to Japan's industry and its people. With the company's continued focus on technology, and with offices throughout the world, the future of Yanmar looks bright.

NOTES

◆ **ll. 3-4 Dr. Rudolf Diesel**　ルドルフ・ディーゼル博士　◆ **l. 12 Magokichi Yamaoka**　山岡孫吉　◆ **ll. 32-33 combine harvester**　コンバイン　◆ **l. 33 rice transplanter**　田植え機　◆ **l. 36 TC500 walk-behind two-row combine**　歩行２条刈コンバイン TC500　◆ **l. 39 TC750 riding two-row reaper**　２条刈コンバイン TC750　◆ **l. 46 YNB300 wheeled mini-excavator**　ホイル式掘削機 YNB300　◆ **l. 47 YFW500 rubber-tracked carrier**　ゴムクローラキャリア（不整地運搬車）YFW500　◆ **l. 59 the Showa Station**　昭和基地

1 Synonym Questions

以下の語句の同意語を選びましょう。単語の左側の数字はその語句が出てくる本文の段落番号です。

1. **1** operate　　＿＿＿＿＿＿＿＿
2. **2** rely　　　　＿＿＿＿＿＿＿＿
3. **2** expensive　＿＿＿＿＿＿＿＿
4. **2** commodity　＿＿＿＿＿＿＿＿
5. **2** hit　　　　 ＿＿＿＿＿＿＿＿
6. **3** damage　　 ＿＿＿＿＿＿＿＿
7. **4** uneven　　 ＿＿＿＿＿＿＿＿
8. **4** carry out　＿＿＿＿＿＿＿＿
9. **5** vital　　　＿＿＿＿＿＿＿＿
10. **5** personnel　＿＿＿＿＿＿＿＿

| bumpy | essential | item | success | costly |
| handle | perform | count | harm | staff |

2 Questions & Answers

質問の答えとして正しいものを一つ選びましょう。

1. How were the first diesel engines?

    (A) It was difficult to operate them.

    (B) They were driven by steam.

    (C) They were small-sized.

2. What was NOT introduced in the 1960s?

    (A) The TC 500

    (B) The YB 1200

    (C) The YNB 300

3. What was the most suitable to carry building materials on rough ground?

    (A) The TC 750

    (B) The YFW 500

    (C) The YNB 300

3 Comprehension Check

本文の内容に合うものを一つ選びましょう。

1. ①～②段落に関して
   (A) In the 19th century, diesel engines were the only means of transporting people and goods.
   (B) Magokichi Yamaoka took a few years to make diesel engines operate at low speeds.
   (C) Small diesel engines indirectly helped people get food at a cheaper price.
   (D) When diesel engines were invented, steam engines had already decreased in popularity.

2. ③～④段落に関して
   (A) The YNB 300 was useful for places where the ground would have previously been dug up by hand.
   (B) When Yanmar released the TC 500, combine harvesters had already been equipped with diesel engines.
   (C) With Japan's rapid economic growth, Yanmar switched from producing construction equipment.
   (D) Yanmar became much stronger than before because it wasn't affected by World War II.

3. ⑤～⑥段落に関して
   (A) It is very important in Antarctica that the power supply system keeps on functioning.
   (B) The range of business Yanmar conducts is relatively narrow.
   (C) Yanmar hasn't expanded overseas except for offering its generators to the Showa Station.
   (D) Yanmar's staff who are stationed at the Showa Station have technicians maintain its generators.

4 Composition

あなたが興味をもっている企業についてホームページなどで事実を調べ、例文を参考にして以下の空欄にあてはまる語句を入れて、その企業の説明を英語でしてみましょう。参照する企業は、例文ごとに変えても、すべて同じ企業でもかまいません。

例1 In the second half of the 20th century, Yanmar diversified into construction equipment.
20世紀後半に、ヤンマーは建設機械の分野にも参入した。

企業名 _____

In (　　　　), (　　　　　) diversified into (　　　　　).

例2 Yanmar has released many types of mini-excavator, including the very popular YB1200 mini-excavator.
ヤンマーは、大人気のYB1200を含むさまざまな種類の小型掘削機を発売してきた。

企業名 _____

(　　　　　) has released many types of (　　　　　), including (　　　　　).

例3 Yanmar's business activities range from small agricultural machinery to extremely large engines used in the South Pole.
ヤンマーの事業活動は小型農業機械類から南極で使用されている巨大エンジンまで及んでいる。

企業名 _____

(　　　　　)'s business activities range from (　　　　　) to (　　　　　).

5 Chronological Table

本文の内容に基づいて、以下の年表を完成させましょう。

年　号	出　来　事
19世紀末	（①　　　　）博士が（①　　　　）エンジンを発明する。
（②　　　）	（③　　　　）が世界初の小型（①　　　　）エンジンを開発し、販売する。
（④　　　）	（①　　　　）エンジンを搭載したホイル式（⑤　　　　）のYNB300を開発する。
（⑥　　　）	ガソリンを動力源としていた（⑦　　　　）に代わる（①　　　　）を動力源とする（⑦　　　　）のTC500を発売する。
（⑧　　　）	刈り取った米を傷つけずに脱穀できる（⑦　　　　）のTC750を発売する。
（⑨　　　）	小型（⑤　　　　）のミニバックホーYB1200を発売する。
（⑩　　　）	ヤンマーのエンジンが（⑪　　　　）大陸の（⑫　　　　）での動力供給に使われ始める。
現在	小型農業機械、船舶エンジン、建設機器から（⑪　　　　）大陸の巨大エンジンまで、そのビジネスは多岐に及んでいる。

トラクターの変遷

YM273 (1968)

YM1500D (1974)

F535 (1989)

US46R (1996)

EG441 (2009)

YT5113 (2015)

Chapter 10

Magokichi Yamaoka

特集記事 山岡孫吉の生涯

ヤンマー創業者山岡孫吉は、1888年滋賀県で生まれました。尋常高等小学校を卒業後、3円60銭を手に大阪のメリヤス問屋に奉公へ。幾多の困難の後、1921年には、農業用小型石油エンジンを開発し、商標を豊作の使者であるトンボの親玉、オニヤンマにちなみ「ヤンマー」としました。1932年、ドイツのメッセで出会ったディーゼルエンジンの優秀さに心をひかれ、帰国後、小型ディーゼルエンジンの製作に没頭します。度重なる失敗を重ね、1933年12月23日、ついに世界初の小型ディーゼルエンジンの開発に成功したのです。

Grammar Tips for the TOEIC® L&R Test

代名詞の格を答える設問に注意しよう。

本文では以下の表現が見られます。

Yamaoka's father had to work a second job as a carpenter to provide for his large family.

上の例では、前置詞 for と名詞のかたまり large family のあいだに入る、Yamaoka's father の代名詞は、him などではなく、やはり his です。

例題を見てみましょう。

> Your subscription to (　　) weekly magazine expires with the current issue.
> (A) our
> (B) ours
> (C) ourselves
> (D) us

(B) の所有代名詞、(C) の再帰代名詞、そして、(D) の代名詞の目的格は、それぞれ前置詞の後ろに入れることができます。しかし、そうすると、to ours、to ourselves、to us という「前置詞＋名詞」のひとかたまりが完結してしまい、そのあとに続く名詞のかたまり weekly magazine が、文の中で浮いてしまうことになります。したがって、名詞の前に形容詞のように入れることができる (A) の代名詞の所有格を選択し、our weekly magazine という名詞のかたまりをつくります。TOEIC® L&R では、代名詞の格の設問では、この例題のように所有格を答えさせるパターンが多く見られます。

Vocabulary Questions

以下の語句の意味を、下の語群から選びましょう。

1. award _____
2. construct _____
3. devote _____
4. donate _____
5. efficient _____
6. enhance _____
7. enterprise _____
8. exhibition _____
9. extremely _____
10. foundation _____
11. huge _____
12. industrial _____
13. installation _____
14. machinery _____
15. outgrow _____
16. premises _____
17. realize _____
18. repair _____
19. run _____
20. statue _____

像	機械類	とても	～を寄付する
企業	展示会	～に気づく	～を建設する
敷地	産業の	～を高める	～を修理する
設置	効率の良い	～をささげる	～を授与する
創立	非常に大きな	～を運営する	～よりも成長する

Language in Use

Audio 2-03

音声を聴いて空欄を埋めましょう。さらに、完成した文の日本語訳を下線部に書きましょう。

1. John finished his day's work and (　　　　)(　　　　)(　　　　) home.

   _____

2. Onomichi City is (　　　　)(　　　　)(　　　　) "the little Kyoto in Setouchi district."

   _____

3. The company (　　　　)(　　　　)(　　　　) a new supplier of office equipment.

   _____

Reading

 Audio 2-04

1 In 2012, Yanmar celebrated its 100th year in business. This company can be traced back to its establishment by Magokichi Yamaoka, a young man from a small town in Shiga Prefecture who had big dreams.

2 Yamaoka was born in 1888 in the northern part of Shiga Prefecture (present day Nagahama). His father ran a small farm, and Magokichi saw how much hard work was involved. In winter, the area was always covered in snow. Due to this, when spring finally came, the land was less fertile than some other parts of Japan. Many of the farmers in the area were extremely poor, and had to work very hard to make a living. Indeed, Yamaoka's father had to work a second job as a carpenter to provide for his large family. Yamaoka was the ninth child of ten. Like many other children at the time, Yamaoka finished school after graduating elementary school, and was expected to work from then.

3 At the age of 15, Yamaoka set off for Osaka. His mother sold a bag of rice in order for Yamaoka to have 3 yen 60 sen for his trip. When he arrived there, he stayed with his older brother. At the time, Osaka was a growing industrial city, sometimes referred to as the "Manchester of the East" because of all the manufacturers based there.

4 Eventually, he found work installing pipes for a gas company. That led to his installing gas engines, through which he began to study how engines worked.

5 In 1906, he started up his own gas pipe installation and equipment sales business, and saved enough money to start his own company in Kita-ku, Osaka called "Yamaoka Gasu Shokai." When the new company had outgrown its premises, Yamaoka leased a large piece of land in Chayamachi, Kita-ku to construct a new company building. He named this new company "Yamaoka Hatsudoki Kosakusho" which officially opened on March 22nd, 1912. This became Yanmar's foundation day. The present day head office of Yanmar is still in the same place.

6 The new company initially repaired and sold gas engines. However, Yamaoka did not forget watching his parents toil on the farm in his childhood. Instead of buying and selling other people's products, he set about designing a completely new engine, one that would make farm work easier. This led to the development of a lighter engine, which the company called the "Yanmar throttle governed oil engine," in 1921. The Yanmar brand had been born!

7 In 1929, Yamaoka saw a diesel engine for the first time at an exhibition in Osaka. In 1932, he traveled to a major trade show in Germany, where seeing the diesel engine again, he began to wonder if it could be made smaller to fit into farm machinery. After returning to Japan, he and his engineers set about creating a smaller version of the diesel engine. They

tried and tried, and met with failure many times. Finally, on December 23rd, 1933, after 17 months, the small diesel engine was born. It could be fitted to farm machinery, and it made farmers' jobs a lot more efficient.

8 On his second trip to Germany in 1953, Yamaoka realized that there was no statue in Germany to commemorate the creator of the diesel engine, Rudolf Diesel. Yamaoka decided that he wanted to fund a memorial to Dr. Diesel in the city of Augsburg. In 1957, after continuing to build relations between Japan and Germany, Yamaoka was awarded the German Cross of the Order of Merit, an extremely high

honor. In the same year, rather than a statue, Yamaoka donated a Japanese stone garden to the city of Augsburg in Germany to commemorate Rudolf Diesel.

9 After devoting his life to Yanmar, Yamaoka passed away in 1962 at the age of 73. He had enhanced Diesel's idea of an engine to provide an extremely efficient way of carrying out farm work. As Diesel's son had told Yamaoka at a meeting in 1954, "It was my departed father's earnest desire to provide a small, efficient engine to small-scale enterprises, and your efforts accomplished what he set out to do."

NOTES

- l. 17 a bag of rice 米1俵 ◆ l. 21 Manchester of the East 東洋のマンチェスター
- l. 28 Yamaoka Gasu Shokai 山岡瓦斯商会 ◆ l. 31 Yamaoka Hatsudoki Kosakusho 山岡発動機工作所 ◆ l. 41 Yanmar throttle governed oil engine ヤンマー変量式石油発動機 ◆ l. 58 the German Cross of the Order of Merit ドイツ大功労十字章

1 Synonym Questions

以下の語句の同意語を選びましょう。単語の左側の数字はその語句が出てくる本文の段落番号です。

1. **2** run _____
2. **2** provide for _____
3. **4** eventually _____
4. **6** repair _____
5. **6** completely _____
6. **7** exhibition _____
7. **8** statue _____
8. **8** commemorate _____
9. **8** award _____
10. **9** enhance _____

| fair | grant | manage | totally | finally |
| honor | sculpture | fix | increase | support |

2 Questions & Answers

質問の答えとして正しいものを一つ選びましょう。

1. What is true about Magokichi Yamaoka?
    (A) He had many younger brothers and sisters.
    (B) He was born in an area with a mild climate.
    (C) His father was a farmer and a carpenter.

2. What is true about Yamaoka Hatsudoki Kosakusho?
    (A) It sold its own products from the start.
    (B) It was established far from where the headquarters now is.
    (C) The land where its building stood was rented.

3. What did Yamaoka do in 1957?
    (A) He built relations between Japan and Germany.
    (B) He established a prize in memory of Rudolf Diesel.
    (C) He gave something to the city of Augsburg.

3 Comprehension Check

本文の内容に合うものを一つ選びましょう。

1. ①〜④段落に関して
   (A) As soon as he arrived in Osaka, Yamaoka worked for a gas company.
   (B) The land in the area where Yamaoka was born was very productive.
   (C) Yamaoka earned money for his travel expenses to Osaka by himself.
   (D) Yanmar celebrated the centennial of its foundation in 2012.

2. ⑤〜⑥段落に関して
   (A) The day when Yamaoka opened Yamaoka Gasu Shoukai became Yanmar's foundation day.
   (B) The scale of Yamaoka's company became so large that it relocated to Chayamachi.
   (C) The Yanmar brand had already been established when a lighter engine was developed in 1921.
   (D) Yamaoka borrowed money and established Yamaoka Gasu Shoukai in 1906.

3. ⑦〜⑨段落に関して
   (A) Diesel's son told Yamaoka that his father invented a small, efficient diesel engine thanks to Yamaoka's efforts.
   (B) It was not until Yamaoka visited Germany that he saw a diesel engine for the first time.
   (C) Yamaoka began creating a smaller diesel engine, and it was completed within a year.
   (D) Yamaoka provided money to establish something to remind people of Dr. Diesel.

4 Composition

あなたが興味をもっている企業についてホームページなどで事実を調べ、例文を参考にして以下の空欄にあてはまる語句を入れて、その企業の説明を英語でしてみましょう。参照する企業は、例文ごとに変えても、すべて同じ企業でもかまいません。

例1 In 2012, Yanmar celebrated its 100th year in business.
2012年に、ヤンマーは創業100周年を祝った。

企業名 _____
In (　　　　), (　　　　　) celebrated (　　　　　) in business.

例2 Magokichi Yamaoka was born in 1888 in the northern part of Shiga Prefecture.
山岡孫吉は1888年に滋賀県北部で生誕した。

企業名 _____
(　　　　　) was born in (　　　　　) in (　　　　　).

例3 March 22nd, 1912 became Yanmar's foundation day.
1912年3月22日がヤンマーの創立記念日となった。

企業名 _____
(　　　　　) became (　　　　　)'s foundation day.

Chronological Table

本文の内容に基づいて、以下の年表を完成させましょう。

年　号	出　来　事
（①　　　）	山岡孫吉が滋賀県長浜市で生誕する。
1903 年	大阪に出て、（②　　　　　）で働き始める。
（③　　　）	大阪市北区で山岡瓦斯商会を開設する。
（④　　　）	3 月 22 日に大阪市北区茶屋町で（⑤　　　　　）を創業する。
（⑥　　　）	初の「ヤンマー」ブランド製品であるヤンマー変量式石油発動機を開発する。
1929 年	大阪の展示会で（⑦　　　　）を初めて目にする。
1932 年	（⑧　　　　　）の見本市で再び（⑦　　　　）を目にし、帰国後、小型の（⑦　　　　）の製作に取りかかる。
（⑨　　　）	12 月 23 日に小型（⑦　　　　）が完成する。
（⑩　　　）	大功労十字章を授与される。アウグスブルグ市に（⑪　　　　）博士の功績を称える（⑪　　　　）記念石庭苑を寄贈する。
（⑫　　　）	73 歳で永眠する。
2012 年	山岡孫吉が人生をささげたヤンマーは創業 100 周年を迎える。

石油発動機組立工場での作業風景（1929 年頃）

山岡孫吉氏（右）大功労十字章授与の様子

Chapter 11 Otafuku Sauce
オタフクソース

企業紹介

オタフクソースは、「食を通じて『健康と豊かさと和』をもたらし、笑顔あふれる社会に寄与」するという理念のもと、ソースやお酢、たれなどの調味料の製造・販売を行っています。2017年には、マレーシア工場で製造し、マレーシアJAKIMより認証を受けたハラール認証調味料を発売。お好み焼とともに成長してきた企業として、栄養価が高く団らんの和を生み出すお好み焼の魅力を広めるため、日本国内外で現地に根差した普及活動にも取り組んでいます。

Grammar Tips for the TOEIC® L&R Test

2つの「主語＋動詞」をつなぐのは、前置詞や副詞ではなく接続詞です。

本文では以下の表現が見られます。

> **Although** Sasaki Shouten **was completely destroyed** by the bomb, in 1946, **he resumed** production of his "Otafuku Vinegar."

he resumed という「主語＋動詞」がそろっている文に、Sasaki Shouten was destroyed という「主語＋動詞」のかたまりをくっつけることができるのは接続詞である although です。although と意味が似ていても、前置詞句 in spite of や副詞 however では、2つの「主語＋動詞」の文をつなぐことはできません。

例題を見てみましょう。

> (　　) clothes you purchase don't fit you, you can send them back to us free of charge.
> 　(A) Because of
> 　(B) If
> 　(C) Instead of
> 　(D) Nevertheless

(A)や(C)の前置詞句や(D)の副詞では、clothes don't fit というような「主語＋動詞」のセットを、you can send というもう一つの「主語＋動詞」のセットにくっつけていくことはできません。したがって、ここでは(B)の接続詞が正答となります。この例題では、選択肢に接続詞がひとつしかないので、文の意味を考えずに正答を選択することができます。

Vocabulary Questions

以下の語句の意味を、下の語群から選びましょう。

1. add　　　　　　_____
2. amount　　　　_____
3. customer　　　_____
4. employee　　　_____
5. establish　　　 _____
6. expansion　　 _____
7. include　　　　_____
8. incredibly　　 _____
9. line　　　　　　_____
10. manage　　　 _____
11. numerous　　_____
12. pan　　　　　 _____
13. produce　　　_____
14. production　　_____
15. provide　　　 _____
16. relatively　　 _____
17. resume　　　 _____
18. satisfied　　　_____
19. shortage　　　_____
20. spread　　　　_____

量	不足	比較的	～を製造する
拡大	平なべ	信じられないほど	～を設立する
顧客	従業員	広がる	～を提供する
商品	数多くの	～を足す	何とか～する
生産	満足して	～を含む	～を再び始める

Language in Use Audio 2-05

音声を聴いて空欄を埋めましょう。さらに、完成した文の日本語訳を下線部に書きましょう。

1. Once the food (　　　)(　　　)(　　　)(　　　)(　　　) air, it starts to go bad.

   _____

2. Most of (　　　)(　　　)(　　　)(　　　)(　　　) the development of this technology.

   _____

3. The newly introduced item is very popular, (　　　)(　　　)(　　　) (　　　)(　　　).

   _____

Reading

1 Otafuku Sauce Co., Ltd. is a Hiroshima based company, first established in 1922 by Seiichi Sasaki, a young man who started selling Japanese sake and soy sauce. He opened a small store called "Sasaki Shouten," and in 1938 began to produce original vinegar. This was sold as "Otafuku Vinegar" and the Otafuku brand was born.

2 Sasaki believed that the products he made for his customers should be safe and delicious. Hiroshima was heavily damaged by the atomic bomb in 1945, but the people worked hard to quickly rebuild their city. Although Sasaki Shouten was completely destroyed by the bomb, in 1946, he resumed production of his "Otafuku Vinegar," and kept true to his motto, "Put everything you've got into each drop, keep the natural flavor, and make sure it's safe." Sasaki really wanted people to be able to eat his products without worrying about their health.

3 After World War II there was a shortage of rice in some areas, especially where there was great damage from the war. This led to the popularity of "Issen-Yoshoku," the forerunner of Okonomiyaki, which could be made using flour that was relatively easy to find, as it was largely provided by other countries. Issen-Yoshoku, meaning "one-coin western food," gradually became a symbol of the city's postwar reconstruction. Initially, it was considered to be a children's snack. Then owners of the places that served Issen-Yoshoku in downtown Hiroshima started to make small adaptations to it, by adding cabbage, eggs, noodles, and a strip of pork to it so that even adults could feel satisfied with the amount. They also changed the name to "Okonomiyaki," and it became a popular dish.

4 As western-style dishes became popular, the company introduced "Otafuku Worcestershire Sauce" in 1950. Okonomiyaki was also eaten with this Worcestershire Sauce. However, the sauce was quite watery, and therefore, readily evaporated when it came into contact with the hot pan (griddle) used to cook. Having heard this from the restaurant owners who were selling Okonomiyaki, after much trial and error, the company introduced "Otafuku Okonomiyaki

Sauce" in 1952. This newly launched sauce was thicker and could remain on the food.

[5] Okonomiyaki rapidly spread throughout Japan, and Otafuku Sauce Co. also grew, expanding their line of products to include "Yakisoba Sauce" in 1960, and "Takoyaki Sauce" in 1964. A lot of hard work went into the research and development of these sauces, and the company managed to become one of the manufacturers of Japan's most-loved sauces.

[6] Otafuku Sauce Co. also has a presence outside of Japan, which began in 1998, when it established their North American branch, now known as Otafuku Foods, in Torrance, California. Initially this was just an office, but in 2013 the company moved to Santa Fe Springs in California, and set up a factory and warehouse, as well as an administration office. At the same time, the company established a production base in China, and now makes products to meet the demands of local people, but also introduces Japanese food, of course with a focus on Okonomiyaki.

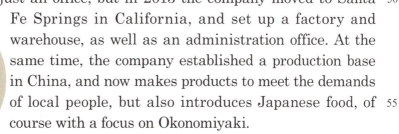

[7] Continuing this overseas expansion, in 2016 the company established OTAFUKU SAUCE MALAYSIA SDN. BHD., a joint venture company. The goal is to allow people all over the world to enjoy Okonomiyaki, irrespective of race or religion. In Malaysia many people do not eat pork or drink alcohol for religious reasons. Using *umami* from fish, the company manufactures HALAL seasonings, including "Okonomi Sauce." In order for the sauce to attain the HALAL certification, all materials used must also have HALAL certification. It is incredibly time-consuming to ensure that all materials are suitable, but Japanese and Malaysian employees work together to ensure that the sauce is made.

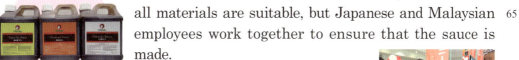

[8] The founder of Otafuku Sauce Co., Seiichi Sasaki, believed that you should never compromise the quality of ingredients, and that every drop counts. Although several generations have passed, these continue to be the governing principles of the company.

NOTES
◆ l. 2 Seiichi Sasaki　佐々木清一　◆ l. 5 Sasaki Shouten　佐々木商店
◆ l. 7 Otafuku Vinegar　お多福酢　◆ ll. 13-15 "Put everything ... safe."　「一滴一滴に性根を込めて、自然の美味しさと安全・安心を追求する」　◆ l. 19 Issen-Yoshoku　一銭洋食　◆ ll. 25-26 owners of the places that served...to it　戦後、広島市内にお好み焼を売る屋台や店が増え始め、その後自宅の一部を改装して店にしたものも出てきた。
◆ ll. 31-32 Otafuku Worcestershire Sauce　オタフクウスターソース

1 Synonym Questions

以下の語句の同意語を選びましょう。単語の左側の数字はその語句が出てくる本文の段落番号です。

1. ① brand _____
2. ② true _____
3. ③ shortage _____
4. ③ relatively _____
5. ③ satisfied _____
6. ③ amount _____
7. ④ readily _____
8. ④ thick _____
9. ⑤ spread _____
10. ⑥ set up _____

| comparatively | expand | lack | quickly | content |
| heavy | loyal | establish | label | quantity |

2 Questions & Answers

質問の答えとして正しいものを一つ選びましょう。

1. What did Seiichi Sasaki mainly sell in 1922?

    (A) Soy sauce

    (B) Vinegar

    (C) Worcestershire sauce

2. Why did Issen-Yoshoku become popular after the war?

    (A) Children liked to eat cheaper food than adults did.

    (B) Its main ingredient was easy to get.

    (C) People liked western food more.

3. Why is it difficult for the company's sauce to get HALAL certification?

    (A) It takes a long time to ensure that all of its ingredients are acceptable.

    (B) Malaysians don't eat pork, so they don't eat Okonomiyaki very often.

    (C) *Umami* from fish doesn't have the same taste as that from pork.

Comprehension Check

本文の内容に合うものを一つ選びましょう。

1. ①～②段落に関して
   (A) As soon as Seiichi founded his company, he started to sell the Otafuku brand.
   (B) One year after Hiroshima was seriously damaged, Seiichi began to produce his vinegar again.
   (C) Sasaki Shouten escaped from the destruction of World War II.
   (D) Seiichi emphasized safety more than taste when he made his product.

2. ③～⑤段落に関して
   (A) Okonomiyaki became a symbol of Hiroshima before the war.
   (B) Okonomiyaki is said to have come from Issen-Yoshoku.
   (C) "Otafuku Worcestershire Sauce" was perfect for Okonomiyaki.
   (D) The company focused on producing its Okonomiyaki Sauce in the 1960s.

3. ⑥～⑦段落に関して
   (A) As they are passed on down the generations, Otafuku Sauce's governing principles have been changing.
   (B) In China, the company devotes itself entirely to producing what local people like.
   (C) Otafuku Foods relocated their office, factory, and warehouse to Santa Fe Springs.
   (D) Otafuku Sauce wants to see people all over the world enjoying Okonomiyaki regardless of their beliefs.

4 Composition

あなたが興味をもっている企業についてホームページなどで事実を調べ、例文を参考にして以下の空欄にあてはまる語句を入れて、その企業の説明を英語でしてみましょう。参照する企業は、例文ごとに変えても、すべて同じ企業でもかまいません。

例 1 Otafuku Sauce is a Hiroshima based company, first established in 1922 by Seiichi Sasaki.

オタフクソースは広島を本拠地とする会社で、佐々木清一によって1922年に創業された。

企業名 _____

(　　　　　) is a (　　　　　　) based company, first established in (　　　　　) by (　　　　　).

例 2 The original vinegar was sold as "Otafuku Vinegar" and the Otafuku brand was born.

オリジナルの酢は「お多福酢」として販売され、お多福ブランドが誕生した。

企業名 _____

(　　　　　) was sold as (　　　　　) and the (　　　　　) brand was born.

例 3 The company expanded their line of sauces to include Yakisoba Sauce in 1960, and Takoyaki Sauce in 1964.

会社はソース商品を拡げ、1960年に「焼そばソース」を、1964年に「たこ焼ソース」を付け加えた。

企業名 _____

(　　　　　) expanded their line of (　　　　　) to include (　　　　　) and (　　　　　).

Chronological Table

本文の内容に基づいて、以下の年表を完成させましょう。

年　　号	出　来　事
（①　　　）	佐々木清一が（②　　　　　）で日本酒や醤油を販売する「佐々木商店」として創業する。
（③　　　）	初のお多福ブランド商品である（④　　　　　）を製造する。
（⑤　　　）	原子爆弾により「佐々木商店」は全壊したが、（④　　　　　）の製造を再開する。
1950年	（⑥　　　　　）を発売する。
（⑦　　　）	新商品「お好み焼用ソース」を発売する。
1960年	「（⑧　　　　　）ソース」を発売する。
1964年	「（⑨　　　　　）ソース」を発売する。
（⑩　　　）	カリフォルニアのトランスに北米事業所（現：Otafuku Foods）を設立する。
2013年	Otafuku Foodsをカリフォルニアのサンタフェスプリングスに移転し、工場と倉庫を併設する。さらに、（⑪　　　　　）にも生産拠点を設立する。
2016年	合弁会社（⑫　　　　　）を設立する。
現在	「一滴一滴に性根を込めて、自然の美味しさと安全・安心を追求する」という創業者のものづくりの心を大切にして、事業を続けている。

お好みソースの変遷

① 1952年　新製品「お好み焼用ソース」発売
② 1957年　「オタフクお好みソース」発売 ※初の家庭用商品
③ 1979年　紙パック容器での販売を開始
④ 1982年　エバール樹脂を使用した「フクボトル」容器を採用
⑤ 1983年　オタフクの商品と認知頂けるよう従来の山型デザインに
⑥ 多少のデザイン変更はありつつも、このパッケージが定着
⑦ 2018年　より分かりやすく、パッケージをリニューアル

Chapter 12

Tombow
トンボ学生服

企業紹介
トンボ学生服は、岡山を拠点に、全国の中高生向けの制服や体育着を製造しているユニフォームメーカーです。日本に学校制服が誕生して既に100年以上が経ちますが、TOMBOWブランドの原点は「生徒の成長を見守る」こと。そして「良い制服を正しく着る」という精神を伝えることで、社会の中でのアイデンティティを芽生えさせ、彼らの明るい未来をつくるお手伝いをすることを目指します。

Grammar Tips for the TOEIC® L&R Test

動詞の前または後ろに入って動詞を修飾する副詞に気をつけよう。

本文では以下の表現が見られます。

Tombow has been able to provide this service effectively.

上の例では様態の副詞 effectively が動詞の後ろに入り、動詞 be able to provide を修飾して、「どのように」なされるのかを示します。

例題を見てみましょう。

> The government (　) insisted on the need for tax reform.
> (A) repeat
> (B) repeated
> (C) repeatedly
> (D) repetition

ここでは、「動詞の前または後ろで動詞を修飾する」という、最もシンプルな副詞の用法を問うており、動詞 insist を修飾する副詞 (C) を選択します。
もちろん、空欄の直前の名詞が形容詞用法の名詞で、空欄には名詞が入るという場合があるので注意が必要ですが、ここでは、(A) や (D) の名詞では文意が通じません。
TOEIC® L&R では、この例題のように、みなさんにとってはかなり易しい文法問題もいくつか出題されますので、むずかしく考えすぎないようにしましょう。

Vocabulary Questions

以下の語句の意味を、下の語群から選びましょう。

1. advanced　　　_____
2. apparel　　　_____
3. educational　　_____
4. effectively　　_____
5. encourage　　_____
6. exhibit　　　_____
7. field　　　　_____
8. focus　　　　_____
9. identify　　　_____
10. launch　　　_____
11. manufacture　_____
12. measure　　　_____
13. overseas　　_____
14. profitable　_____
15. renowned　　_____
16. require　　_____
17. tailor　　　_____
18. traditional　_____
19. unique　　　_____
20. vary　　　_____

衣服	展示品	伝統的な	～を測る
焦点	進んだ	利益をもたらす	～を奨励する
発売	独特な	海外で	～を製造する
分野	有名な	効果的に	～を特定する
仕立屋	教育の	さまざまである	～を必要とする

Language in Use

🔊 Audio 2-07

音声を聴いて空欄を埋めましょう。さらに、完成した文の日本語訳を下線部に書きましょう。

1. (　　　)(　　　)(　　　)(　　　) presidents reported instances of poverty in their childhood.

   _____

2. The development of the equipment (　　　)(　　　)(　　　)(　　　) the company.

   _____

3. Susan (　　　)(　　　)(　　　)(　　　) a strong candidate for mayor.

   _____

Reading

1. School uniforms are a common sight in everyday life in Japan. Up to 95% of high schools in Japan require students to wear a uniform, and most junior high schools do too. An interesting fact is that most of these uniforms are made in Okayama. In fact, seven out of ten Japanese school uniforms are made in that prefecture. Okayama is also the home of Tombow Co., Ltd, Japan's leading uniform maker. Tombow was established in 1876 by Kumagoro Miyake, as a manufacturer of *tabi*, which are Japanese socks with a split toe. In the next century though, it would become renowned for making school uniforms.

2. In the late 1800s, school uniforms were only starting to be introduced at schools throughout Japan. Traditionally, students had worn kimono, but after the beginning of the Meiji period, Western-style uniforms began to become popular. For boys, the *gakuran* style was popular, which was based on military uniforms from Prussia. The *tsume-eri* style was another, based on navy uniforms. Apparently, the navy had a romantic image for many people in Japan at the time, because sailors could travel overseas.

3. For girls, the "sailor" outfit became popular. The first one-piece sailor style uniform can be traced back to the beginning of the 20th century. However, the introduction of the modern two-piece sailor uniform is generally credited to Kinjo Girls' School in Aichi and Fukuoka Girls' School in Fukuoka in 1921. It is said that in Fukuoka Girls' School, Elizabeth Lee, the then American headmistress, had an idea for a two-piece sailor design, and asked a local tailor to design it. It then became the blueprint for the uniform still worn by millions of girls in Japan today.

4. Originally, school uniforms were made by small local tailors. However, that changed at the very beginning of the 1930s. Tombow was still making *tabi* at the time, but the company was struggling to make enough money from *tabi* sales alone. Now they saw a huge opportunity in the new field.

People were encouraged to have a lot of children (many families had six to eight), and the Japanese government was increasing educational opportunities for children. Therefore, Tombow identified a very big and growing market — school uniforms. In 1930, they started to manufacture school uniforms, and from that time on, they have gone from strength to strength. After World War II, the baby boom meant that the company became even more profitable.

5 In 1965, they introduced a washable student uniform for the first time. In the 1970s, Tombow diversified into other products, such as the launch of its Victory sportswear range in 1977.

6 One of the reasons that Tombow has remained a popular maker of uniforms is its focus on good design. For example, in 1989, the fashion designer Kansai Yamamoto created new school uniform designs for the company. Tombow has also collaborated with other designers for other kinds of uniforms, for example Yumi Katsura's designs for women's office uniforms in 1990. In addition, the company has worked together with other apparel companies, such as its collaboration with "OLIVE des OLIVE," which began in 2003.

7 In 1996, Tombow opened Japan's only academic uniform museum. At the museum, visitors can see exhibits of uniforms both from Japan and some other parts of the world. They can also find out how uniforms have changed over time. The museum has many historically important artifacts, such as original Japanese school uniforms from the Meiji era, and traditional school uniforms from famous British schools. One very interesting exhibit is a photo of a schoolgirl from St Agnes' School in Kyoto, and this has been identified as the first time a sailor-style one-piece uniform was used. Visitors to the museum can learn not only the way uniform fashion has changed, but also about history in general.

8 Each school has its own unique uniform design, and of course, the sizes of the uniforms vary. Usually, each student's size is measured in February or March (after it has been decided which school they will enter) and their uniforms must be ready by the time the students enter their new school. Therefore, there is a very short time between receiving uniform orders and sending them to students. With years of experience and the help of advanced technology, Tombow has been able to provide this service effectively, and makes sure that all new students are able to wear their brand-new uniforms on the day of the entrance ceremony at their new school.

NOTES ◆ l. 9 Kumagoro Miyake 三宅熊五郎 ◆ ll. 23-24 Kinjo Girls' School 金城女学校 ◆ l. 24 Fukuoka Girls' School 福岡女学校 ◆ l. 25 Elizabeth Lee エリザベス・リー ◆ l. 46 Kansai Yamamoto 山本寛斎 ◆ l. 48 Yumi Katsura 桂由美 ◆ l. 50 OLIVE des OLIVE オリーブ・デ・オリーブ ◆ l. 61 St Agnes' School 平安女学院

1 Synonym Questions

以下の語句の同意語を選びましょう。単語の左側の数字はその語句が出てくる本文の段落番号です。

1. [1] common _____
2. [1] renowned _____
3. [3] blueprint _____
4. [4] struggle _____
5. [4] huge _____
6. [4] identify _____
7. [5] launch _____
8. [6] collaboration _____
9. [7] identify _____
10. [8] vary _____

| cooperation | famous | range | usual | discover |
| introduction | recognize | enormous | model | strive |

2 Questions & Answers

質問の答えとして正しいものを一つ選びましょう。

1. What is true about Western-style school uniforms?

    (A) *Gakuran* was based on navy uniforms.

    (B) "Sailor" was a two-piece style at first.

    (C) *Tsume-eri* impressed people as being romantic.

2. What is NOT a reason that the market for school uniforms grew?

    (A) A baby boom began in postwar Japan.

    (B) Children's chances to be educated increased.

    (C) Small local tailors stopped producing them.

3. What can visitors do at Tombow's museum?

    (A) Follow changes in school uniforms

    (B) Get historically important artifacts

    (C) Have a photo taken in a uniform

98　Chapter 12

3 Comprehension Check

本文の内容に合うものを一つ選びましょう。

1. 1〜2段落に関して
   (A) Even before the Meiji era started, Western-style uniforms had been well received.
   (B) Kumagoro Miyake founded Tombow as a maker of school uniforms.
   (C) More than two thirds of Japanese school uniforms are produced in Okayama.
   (D) We see school uniforms displayed in shop windows every day.

2. 3〜5段落に関して
   (A) Aichi and Fukuoka are said to be the homes of the modern two-piece sailor uniform.
   (B) As soon as Tombow entered the school uniform business, they launched a washable school uniform.
   (C) Elizabeth Lee designed a two-piece sailor uniform and asked a local tailor to make it.
   (D) Tombow easily made enough money by just selling *tabi*.

3. 6〜8段落に関して
   (A) The design of each school's uniform is unique, but sizes are almost the same.
   (B) Tombow has worked in cooperation with some designers, but not with any clothing companies.
   (C) Tombow's long experience enables it to send uniforms to all new students in a very short time.
   (D) Visitors can't see any foreign school uniforms at Tombow's museum.

4 Composition

あなたが興味をもっている企業についてホームページなどで事実を調べ、例文を参考にして以下の空欄にあてはまる語句を入れて、その企業の説明を英語でしてみましょう。参照する企業は、例文ごとに変えても、すべて同じ企業でもかまいません。

例 1 Okayama is the home of Tombow Co., Ltd.
岡山は株式会社トンボの発祥の地である。

企業名 _____
(   ) is the home of (   ).

例 2 Tombow identified a very big and growing market — school uniforms.
トンボは学生服というとても大きくて成長途上の市場を見つけた。

企業名 _____
(   ) identified a (   ) market — (   ).

例 3 In 1996, Tombow opened Japan's only academic uniform museum.
1996年にトンボは日本で唯一のユニフォームミュージアムを開いた。

企業名 _____
In (   ), (   ) opened (   ) museum.

計画・材料調達

裁断

仕上げ

5 Chronological Table

本文の内容に基づいて、以下の年表を完成させましょう。

年　号	出　来　事
（①　　）	三宅熊五郎が（②　　　　）で（③　　　　　　）のメーカーとして創業する。
（④　　）	学生服の製造を開始する。
第二次大戦後	（⑤　　　　　　）の影響もあり、業績を伸ばしていく。
1965 年	（⑥　　　　　）ができる学生服を発売する。
（⑦　　）	ビクトリースポーツウエアを発売する。
1989 年	デザイナー（⑧　　　　　）氏とスクールユニフォームで提携する。
1990 年	デザイナー（⑨　　　　　）氏とレディースオフィスユニフォームで提携する。
（⑩　　）	（⑪　　　　　）ミュージアムを開設する。
2003 年	アパレル会社（⑫　　　　　）と提携する。
現在	短い納期で、ひとりひとりの体形に合わせて仕立てるという特殊な商品を、長年の経験と先進の技術で製造し続けている。

社名とロゴの変遷

社名	ロゴ
三宅商店　1876 年より 帝國足袋株式會社　1924 年より	1910 年より
帝國興業株式會社　1944 年より 帝国興業株式会社　1955 年より テイコク株式会社　1974 年より	1930 年より　1955 年より　トンボ学生服／Tombow 1955 年より 1948 年より　Tombow 1974 年より
テイコク株式会社　1989 年より 株式会社トンボ　2006 年より	TOMBOW 1989 年より トンボ学生服／TOMBOW 2006 年より

Chapter 13

Nitto
日東電工

企業紹介 日東電工は 1918 年の創立以来、時代に先んじてニーズを捉え、ディスプレイ表示用光学フィルムや自動車関連材料、経皮吸収型テープ製剤などの製品を通じて幅広い産業活動を支えている総合部材メーカーです。グループ会社の株式会社ニトムズの製品「コロコロ®」はカーペットや床掃除の必需品として多くの家庭で愛用されています。"Innovation for Customers" をブランドスローガンに掲げ、健やかで快適な暮らしを支えるべく、世界中でイノベーションにチャレンジし続けています。

Grammar Tips for the TOEIC® L&R Test

動名詞を修飾する副詞を入れて、前置詞の後ろに大きな名詞のかたまりを完成させよう。

本文では以下の表現が見られます。

By constantly developing new products, Nitto is now renowned globally as a leading diversified material manufacturer.

上の例では、「新製品を開発すること」という名詞のかたまりをつくる動名詞 developing を、副詞 constantly が修飾しています。その結果、前置詞 by の後ろに、前置詞の目的語としての大きな名詞のかたまりが完成します。

例題を見てみましょう。

> We thank you for (　) demonstrating the use of the new office automation equipment.
>   (A) succeed
>   (B) success
>   (C) successful
>   (D) successfully

まず、動名詞 demonstrating の意味上の主語として、あるいは現在分詞 demonstrating が形容詞的に修飾する名詞として、(B) の名詞が正答の可能性はありますが、ここでは文の意味が通じません。そして、動名詞 demonstrating の後ろに前置詞がないことから、この動名詞は名詞よりも動詞の性質が強いことがわかるので、名詞を修飾する (C) の形容詞ではなく、動詞を修飾する (D) の副詞を選択します。その結果、前置詞 for の目的語として、successfully demonstrating the use of the new office automation equipment「新しい OA 機器の使い方を見事に実演すること」という大きな名詞のかたまりが完成します。

Vocabulary Questions

以下の語句の意味を、下の語群から選びましょう。

1. anniversary　　＿＿＿＿＿＿
2. apply　　＿＿＿＿＿＿
3. attain　　＿＿＿＿＿＿
4. battery　　＿＿＿＿＿＿
5. client　　＿＿＿＿＿＿
6. competitor　　＿＿＿＿＿＿
7. consumer　　＿＿＿＿＿＿
8. crucial　　＿＿＿＿＿＿
9. domain　　＿＿＿＿＿＿
10. dominate　　＿＿＿＿＿＿
11. economic　　＿＿＿＿＿＿
12. electrical　　＿＿＿＿＿＿
13. electricity　　＿＿＿＿＿＿
14. electronics　　＿＿＿＿＿＿
15. global　　＿＿＿＿＿＿
16. rapidly　　＿＿＿＿＿＿
17. relocate　　＿＿＿＿＿＿
18. remove　　＿＿＿＿＿＿
19. strategy　　＿＿＿＿＿＿
20. suitable　　＿＿＿＿＿＿

顧客	記念日	適切な	移転する
戦略	消費者	経済の	優位を占める
電気	競合相手	世界的な	〜に到達する
電池	電子機器	電気に関する	〜を取り外す
領域	急速に	きわめて重要な	〜を適用する

Language in Use　　🔊 Audio 2-09

音声を聴いて空欄を埋めましょう。さらに、完成した文の日本語訳を下線部に書きましょう。

1. That charity concert (　　　)(　　　)(　　　)(　　　) attention and support.

　＿＿＿＿＿＿＿＿＿＿＿＿＿＿＿＿＿＿＿＿＿＿＿＿＿＿＿＿＿＿＿＿＿＿

2. The company (　　　)(　　　)(　　　)(　　　) during the period of rapid economic growth.

　＿＿＿＿＿＿＿＿＿＿＿＿＿＿＿＿＿＿＿＿＿＿＿＿＿＿＿＿＿＿＿＿＿＿

3. John (　　　)(　　　)(　　　)(　　　) his fluency in Japanese at the conference.

　＿＿＿＿＿＿＿＿＿＿＿＿＿＿＿＿＿＿＿＿＿＿＿＿＿＿＿＿＿＿＿＿＿＿

Reading

🔊 Audio 2-10

1 Niche companies generally focus on a small and very specific area, and have some advantages over other companies. The word, "niche," originally comes from French, meaning "space in a wall to display a statue or other ornament." From this definition, the word has also come to mean "a comfortable or suitable place." Nitto is a leading manufacturer in Japan that tries to find its "niche" (comfortable place) in a wide range of business fields, where it has no competitors, and therefore can make most use of its technology to attain top market share.

2 Nitto is probably most well-known for its dominance in niche markets. It tries to find a niche, and then innovates and dominates in that area. An example of this is a polarizing film for LCD, a kind of optical film used in smartphones, computers and televisions. Without this film, the screen will appear blank, so it is a crucial part of any display. Nitto has the top market share for this product. Smartphones might contain other Nitto products, too. For example, there are Nitto's touch sensor materials, adhesive sheets, and micro porous films that are designed to keep dust and water out of your phone, but let air in.

3 Although now based in Osaka, Nitto actually started its life in Tokyo in 1918. It was a time when electricity supply was rapidly spreading through Japan, but electrical equipment and machinery were mostly imported from the West. To aid the supply of domestically produced products, the company began making electrical insulating materials, which are important components of electrical equipment and machinery. In 1945, their Tokyo-based head office was destroyed in an air raid.

4 In 1946, the company relocated to Osaka, and ventured into the domain of adhesive tape by beginning large-scale production of Black Tape, which is insulating tape for electric wires. It also began offering final consumer goods such as batteries and tape recorders under the brand name "Maxell." Then in 1961, after Nitto separated from Maxell, the company took a leap forward as an industrial material manufacturer. In the 1960s the company decided to enter the

field of industrial tapes, a market that was expected to increase in the era of economic growth in Japan. The company then expanded its business to overseas markets, such as the United States and Taiwan.

5 From the 1970s to the 1980s, the company began supplying polarizing films for use in electronics. COLOCOLO®, the now widely used floor cleaner, was also created during this period. With this you can pick up little particles of dust or dirt.

6 Nitto's transdermal drug delivery patches used in hospitals are also worthy of mention. These are patches that you stick to your skin which gradually release drugs into your body. These patches mean that injections are not necessary, and they also remove the need to take medicine orally, which can create problems for those who have difficulties in swallowing. Nitto has been a pioneer in this field since the 1970s.

7 It was in 1996 that Nitto began their business strategy "the Global Niche Top™." The goal is to achieve top market share by applying its unique technology to niche areas. Why the top? By staying in first place, Nitto can get business opportunities from its clients faster than its competitors. The company can then offer the desired product for its customers before the market gets large enough for other competitors to join. By constantly developing new products, Nitto is now renowned globally as a leading diversified material manufacturer. It has about 13,500 different products in more than 70 different areas of business around the world.

8 In 2018, Nitto celebrated its 100th anniversary. With its brand slogan, "Innovations for Customers," Nitto will continue to innovate with its advanced technology, contributing to people's lives in many different ways for the next 100 years.

NOTES

◆ l. 14 polarizing film for LCD　LCD用偏光フィルム　◆ l. 19 micro porous film　マイクロ多孔質フィルム　◆ l. 31 Black Tape　ブラックテープ　◆ ll. 47-48 transdermal drug delivery patches　経皮吸収型テープ製剤　◆ l. 56 the Global Niche Top™　グローバルニッチトップ™

1 Synonym Questions

以下の語句の同意語を選びましょう。単語の左側の数字はその語句が出てくる本文の段落番号です。

1. **1** suitable _____
2. **1** competitor _____
3. **1** attain _____
4. **2** crucial _____
5. **3** relocate _____
6. **4** domain _____
7. **7** client _____
8. **7** constantly _____
9. **7** globally _____
10. **7** diversified _____

| achieve | customer | move | vital | appropriate |
| field | rival | continuously | internationally | varied |

2 Questions & Answers

質問の答えとして正しいものを一つ選びましょう。

1. Which of the following consumer goods is for cleaning?
   (A) Black Tape
   (B) COLOCOLO®
   (C) Polarizing film for LCD

2. What plays the most important part in mobile phone displays?
   (A) Insulating tape
   (B) Polarizing film
   (C) Transdermal drug delivery patches

3. What is most likely to be used in medical treatment?
   (A) Insulating tape
   (B) Polarizing film
   (C) Transdermal drug delivery patches

Comprehension Check

本文の内容に合うものを一つ選びましょう。

1. ①〜②段落に関して
   (A) Niche markets are so small that they provide very little profit.
   (B) Nitto has the top market share for a display used in smartphones, computers, and televisions.
   (C) Nitto is always looking for niches where there are no rivals.
   (D) Nitto's touch sensors keep dust and water out of your smartphone, but let air in.

2. ③〜④段落に関して
   (A) By making electrical insulating materials, Nitto helped the supply of domestically produced electrical appliances.
   (B) Even after separating from Maxell, Nitto continued producing batteries and tape recorders.
   (C) Nitto doubted that it would be successful in the area of tape production.
   (D) Nitto was founded in Osaka in 1918 and has been based there ever since.

3. ⑤〜⑧段落に関して
   (A) According to its business strategy released in 1996, Nitto is motivated to attain top market share.
   (B) By staying in first place, Nitto can provide its customers with what they want, even after other rivals join the growing market.
   (C) Nitto has more than 13 thousand kinds of products in more than 70 different countries around the world.
   (D) Nitto's transdermal drug delivery patches can create problems for those who have difficulties in swallowing.

Composition

あなたが興味をもっている企業についてホームページなどで事実を調べ、例文を参考にして以下の空欄にあてはまる語句を入れて、その企業の説明を英語でしてみましょう。参照する企業は、例文ごとに変えても、すべて同じ企業でもかまいません。

例1 Nitto is probably most well-known for its dominance in niche markets.
Nittoはニッチ市場において優位に立っていることでおそらく最も知られている。

企業名 _____

(   ) is probably most well-known for its dominance in (   ) markets.

例2 It was in 1996 that Nitto began their business strategy "the Global Niche Top™."
1996年にNittoは「グローバルニッチトップ™」というビジネス戦略を開始した。

企業名 _____

It was (   ) that (   ) began their business strategy (   ).

例3 Nitto has about 13,500 different products in more than 70 different areas of business around the world.
Nittoは世界中で70を超えるさまざまなビジネス分野において、13,500ものさまざまな商品を提供している。

企業名 _____

(   ) has (   ) different products in (   ) different areas of business around the world.

5 Chronological Table

本文の内容に基づいて、以下の年表を完成させましょう。

年　号	出　来　事
（①　　　）	東京で創立し、（②　　　　）の生産を始める。
1945 年	（③　　　　）が空襲で破壊される。
1946 年	本社を大阪に移転し、電気絶縁用テープである（④　　　　）の大量生産を始めて、粘着テープ分野に進出する。
1960 年代	（⑤　　　　）テープ分野への進出を決める。アメリカや台湾などの海外市場にも事業を拡大する。
（⑥　　　）	マクセルを切り離し、工業材メーカーとして飛躍を目指す。
1970 年代～ 1980 年代	（⑦　　　　）分野における偏光板、（⑧　　　　）分野における経皮吸収型テープ製剤、フロアクリーナー（⑨　　　　）などの製品が誕生する。
（⑩　　　）	（⑪　　　　）というビジネス戦略を開始する。
2018 年	創立 100 周年を迎える。
現在	（⑫　　　　）というブランドスローガンのもと、人々の暮らしに貢献するビジネス活動を続けている。

ロゴの変遷

Chapter 14

Morozoff
モロゾフ

企業紹介

神戸市東灘区に本社を置く、東証プライム上場の洋菓子メーカー、モロゾフ。『こころつなぐ。笑顔かがやく。』を企業スローガンとし、お客様に心豊かな生活を提案し、常に感動をお届けするためのスイーツを製造・販売しています。全国の百貨店や商業施設で販売店およびカフェ店舗を展開。主力商品はチョコレートやプリン、チーズケーキ、クッキーなど。1932年に日本で初めてバレンタインチョコレートを発売した企業でもあります。

Grammar Tips for the TOEIC® L&R Test

前置詞の後ろには、必ず名詞（のはたらきをするかたまり）が入ります。

本文では以下の表現が見られます。

① It is said that the confectionery company Morozoff is responsible **for introducing** Valentine's Day to Japan in the early 20th century.
② Morozoff adopted glass pots in 1973, which had the advantage **of conveying** the heat slowly into the center of the custard.

①では前置詞 for の後ろに introducing Valentine's Day to Japan in the early 20th century、②では前置詞 of の後ろに conveying the heat slowly into the center of the custard という動名詞を用いた名詞のはたらきをする大きなかたまりが、それぞれ入っています。

例題を見てみましょう。

> Mike is in charge of (　　) the entire division.
> (A) supervising
> (B) supervision
> (C) supervisor
> (D) supervisory

前置詞の後ろには必ずその目的語としての名詞が入るので、空欄の直前の前置詞 of をヒントに (B) や (C) の名詞を選びたくなります。しかし、そのどちらかが正答だとすると、「of ＋名詞」のかたまりが完成してしまい、空欄右側の名詞のかたまり the entire division が行き場を失い、文が成立しません。そこで、(A) の動名詞を選択し、the entire division を supervising の目的語として続くようにします。こうすると、前置詞 of の後ろに「部門全体を監督すること」という意味になる名詞のはたらきをするかたまりができます。TOEIC® L&R ではこの例題のように、動名詞を選択して大きな名詞のかたまりをつくる問題が出題されます。

Vocabulary Questions

以下の語句の意味を、下の語群から選びましょう。

1. advantage　　＿＿＿＿＿＿
2. authentic　　＿＿＿＿＿＿
3. celebrate　　＿＿＿＿＿＿
4. consistently　＿＿＿＿＿＿
5. construction　＿＿＿＿＿＿
6. container　　＿＿＿＿＿＿
7. durability　　＿＿＿＿＿＿
8. exchange　　＿＿＿＿＿＿
9. express　　＿＿＿＿＿＿
10. luxury　　＿＿＿＿＿＿
11. mayor　　＿＿＿＿＿＿
12. purpose　　＿＿＿＿＿＿
13. quality　　＿＿＿＿＿＿
14. rare　　＿＿＿＿＿＿
15. relation　　＿＿＿＿＿＿
16. serve　　＿＿＿＿＿＿
17. share　　＿＿＿＿＿＿
18. square　　＿＿＿＿＿＿
19. surprising　＿＿＿＿＿＿
20. taste　　＿＿＿＿＿＿

質	広場	まれな	～を祝う
好み	目的	高級な	～を出す
関係	容器	本物の	～を分け合う
建設	耐久性	驚くべき	～を交換する
市長	有利な点	首尾一貫して	～を表現する

Language in Use

🔊 Audio 2-11

音声を聴いて空欄を埋めましょう。さらに、完成した文の日本語訳を下線部に書きましょう。

1. The memo from the legal department (　　　)(　　　)(　　　)
   (　　　) for the meeting.

   ＿＿＿＿＿＿＿＿＿＿＿＿＿＿＿＿＿＿＿＿＿＿＿＿＿＿＿＿＿＿

2. (　　　)(　　　)(　　　)(　　　) sales have increased, we should open some new outlets.

   ＿＿＿＿＿＿＿＿＿＿＿＿＿＿＿＿＿＿＿＿＿＿＿＿＿＿＿＿＿＿

3. The division (　　　)(　　　)(　　　)(　　　) the company's annual charity concert.

   ＿＿＿＿＿＿＿＿＿＿＿＿＿＿＿＿＿＿＿＿＿＿＿＿＿＿＿＿＿＿

Reading

1 Most people in Japan enjoy Valentine's Day, by either giving or receiving delicious chocolates and sweets. It is celebrated on February 14th as a day of romance around the world. The history of Valentine's Day goes back to the Middle Ages in Europe when people began exchanging romantic greetings. However, the history of Valentine's Day in Japan is actually quite short. It is said that the confectionery company Morozoff is responsible for introducing Valentine's Day to Japan in the early 20th century.

2 Morozoff is one of Japan's leading luxury confectionery makers, beginning as a chocolate shop in Kobe in 1931. Because chocolate was considered rare and precious in Japan at that time, fancy boxes of chocolates sold at their store became a symbol of wealth and luxury, representing the modernity of the Western way of life. A year later, in 1932, Morozoff introduced Valentine's Day to Japan. They started a custom of giving chocolate on February 14th, with "Sweetheart," an assortment of fancy chocolates, and "Bouquet d'amour," a basket full of flower-shaped chocolates. Ever since then, February 14th has become a day to express love in Japan.

3 From early on, Morozoff has always strived to develop authentic Western-style confectionery products. At the same time, they consider Japanese customers' tastes as well. One product is their custard pudding, now well-known as Morozoff's long selling product. The forerunner of today's Morozoff Custard Pudding was first served at a coffee shop in Tokyo, the Morozoff Nisseki Shop, in 1962. Because the puddings were originally handmade in thick ceramic pots, only a few dozen were available each day. Before long, however, as the pudding became more and more popular, Morozoff embarked on mass production of the puddings in a factory. In order to achieve the same quality and taste of the handmade puddings, the puddings' pots needed

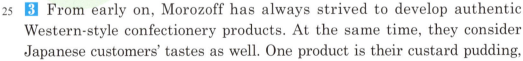

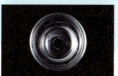

to be strong enough to withstand the process of steam baking. After many years of trial and error, Morozoff adopted glass pots in 1973, which had the advantage of conveying the heat slowly into the center of the custard, enabling the whole pudding to be cooked consistently throughout.

4 Since then, the glass pots have been an indispensable part of the pudding, not only for their original purpose, but also as silent advertisers of the product, even after customers have finished eating them. Due to the pots' durability and compact size, users are able to save and re-use them for a variety of different purposes at home. These pots then remind everyone that sees them of the Morozoff brand.

5 Along with its popular Denmark Cream Cheese Cake, another of Morozoff's well-known confectionery products is the "Arcadia" cookie. Each one of these aromatic cookies contains a large roasted nut. Like the glass pots of the Morozoff Custard Pudding, Arcadia's solid container — a square, golden-colored can with the name printed in the middle — is so popular and well-known that it is hard to find someone who has never seen it.

6 Given the fact that Morozoff has spent many decades developing Western sweets for Japanese tastes, it is probably not surprising that the company has also been involved in building relations with the West. In May 2013, the company funded the construction of a bus stop in "Valentine Square" which is in front of Hanshin Mikage Station. It commemorates the fact that Kobe City was the first place in Japan to initiate a Valentine's Day event. Valentine Square includes a map of Terni City in Italy, where "Saint Valentine" after whom Valentine's Day is named, was born. The mayor of Terni was present at its opening. Thanks to Morozoff's efforts, Kobe City and Terni City now share a strong bond.

NOTES
◆ l. 5 the Middle Ages　中世　◆ l. 21 Sweetheart　スイートハート
◆ l. 22 Bouquet d'amour　ブーケ・ダムール　◆ l. 31 the Morozoff Nisseki Shop　モロゾフ日石ショップ　◆ l. 53 Arcadia　アルカディア　◆ ll. 65-66 Valentine Square　バレンタイン広場　◆ l. 66 Hanshin Mikage Station　阪神御影駅　◆ l. 69 Terni City　テルニ市

Synonym Questions

以下の語句の同意語を選びましょう。単語の左側の数字はその語句が出てくる本文の段落番号です。

1. 2 precious _____
2. 2 custom _____
3. 3 strive _____
4. 3 authentic _____
5. 3 withstand _____
6. 3 advantage _____
7. 4 indispensable _____
8. 4 save _____
9. 6 surprising _____
10. 6 construction _____

| benefit | habit | resist | valuable | building |
| real | struggle | essential | reserve | unexpected |

 Questions & Answers

質問の答えとして正しいものを一つ選びましょう。

1. What did Morozoff introduce one year after its opening?

    (A) Arcadia

    (B) Morozoff Custard Pudding

    (C) Valentine's Day

2. Why did Morozoff change the material of the puddings' pots?

    (A) To improve the taste of the puddings

    (B) To mass-produce the puddings

    (C) To serve the puddings at a coffee shop in Tokyo

3. Where is Valentine Square?

    (A) At the place where Morozoff started its business

    (B) On a map of Terni City, Italy

    (C) In front of Hanshin Mikage Station

Comprehension Check

本文の内容に合うものを一つ選びましょう。

1. 1～2段落に関して
   (A) Morozoff adopted Valentine's Day to start a new custom in Japan.
   (B) Morozoff took several years from when it started to think of a way of selling more chocolates.
   (C) People in Europe exchanged chocolates and sweets on Valentine's Day in the Middle Ages.
   (D) When Morozoff started its business, chocolates had already become something the general public enjoyed in everyday life in Japan.

2. 3～4段落に関して
   (A) Ceramic pots were very effective for mass production of the custard puddings.
   (B) Morozoff has developed Western-style confectionery, leaving its original taste untouched.
   (C) Morozoff was able to adopt glass pots immediately after the decision to change the puddings' containers.
   (D) The long-term effect of the puddings' glass pots is that people remember the Morozoff brand.

3. 5～6段落に関して
   (A) A solid relationship has existed between Kobe and Terni cities due to Morozoff's efforts.
   (B) It is hard to find someone who recognizes the Arcadia container.
   (C) Saint Valentine, who lived in Terni City, named February 14th Valentine's Day.
   (D) The square, golden-colored can of Arcadia stands out though the product name isn't printed on it.

4 Composition

あなたが興味をもっている企業についてホームページなどで事実を調べ、例文を参考にして以下の空欄にあてはまる語句を入れて、その企業の説明を英語でしてみましょう。参照する企業は、例文ごとに変えても、すべて同じ企業でもかまいません。

例 1 Morozoff is one of Japan's leading luxury confectionery makers.
モロゾフは日本のトップの高級菓子メーカーのひとつだ。

企業名 _____
(   ) is one of (   )'s leading (   ).

例 2 In 1932, Morozoff introduced Valentine's Day to Japan.
1932年にモロゾフはバレンタインデーを日本に紹介した。

企業名 _____
In (   ), (   ) introduced (   ) to (   ).

例 3 These pots remind everyone that sees them of the Morozoff brand.
これらの容器はそれを目にする人にモロゾフというブランドを思い出させる。

企業名 _____
(   ) remind everyone (   ) of the (   ) brand.

人気のチーズケーキ（左）とカスタードプリン（右）

5 Chronological Table

本文の内容に基づいて、以下の年表を完成させましょう。

年　号	出　来　事
（①　　）	神戸で（②　　　　）の店として創業する。
（③　　）	（④　　　　　）を日本に紹介し、2月14日に（②　　　　　）を贈る慣習を始める。
1962年	（⑤　　　　　）の前身となる商品が東京の喫茶店モロゾフ日石ショップで提供される。当時の容器は（⑥　　　　　）製であった。
（⑦　　）	（⑤　　　　）に（⑧　　　　　）製の容器を採用する。この容器はモロゾフのクッキー（⑨　　　　）の缶とともに広く認知される容器となっている。
（⑩　　）	阪神御影駅前につくられた（⑪　　　　　）にバス停を寄贈する。そこには（④　　　　　）の名前の由来である聖バレンチノが生誕したイタリアの都市である（⑫　　　　　）市の地図も設置されている。
現在	日本人の好みに合わせた西洋菓子を開発し続けている。

ロゴの変遷

モロゾフのロゴマークはモスクワのクレムリン宮殿にある世界一巨大な鐘をモチーフにしたものです。

創業当初より1972年8月まで使用されていたモロゾフ ロゴマーク

1972年8月以降から1976年まで使用されていたモロゾフ ロゴマーク

モロゾフ製菓株式会社からモロゾフ株式会社に変更

1976年以降から現在使用されているモロゾフ ロゴマーク

Chapter 15

Company Museums and Cafés 特集記事 ミュージアムとカフェ

企業が自社の事業内容や製品について消費者により深く理解してもらうために、工場見学の機会をもうけたり、専用の施設をつくって一般に開放していることがあります。その例として、この最終章では、本教科書に登場するいくつかの会社のミュージアムやカフェを紹介しています。どの施設も、特別なイベントへの参加を除いて、事前予約の手続きなしに訪れることができます。みなさんが興味を持っている企業にも、訪ねていける施設があるかもしれません。本教科書読了後に、ぜひ行ってみましょう。

Grammar Tips for the TOEIC® L&R Test

名詞（のはたらきをするかたまり）を「主語＋動詞」につなぐのは接続詞や副詞ではなく（句）前置詞だ。

本文では以下の表現が見られます。

Information about roasting techniques is also available, as well as tips about the best ways to prepare and enjoy coffee.

Information ... is と「主語＋動詞」がそろっている文に、tips about the best ways to prepare and enjoy coffee という名詞のはたらきをする大きなかたまりをくっつけることは、because のような接続詞や therefore のような副詞にはできません。ここでは、as well as のような（句）前置詞が必要となります。

例題を見てみましょう。

> The trains have all been delayed (　　) a signal breakdown between Kyoto and Osaka this morning.
> 　(A) as a result
> 　(B) due to
> 　(C) even though
> 　(D) in spite of

空欄の左側には trains have been delayed というように「主語＋動詞」がそろっていますが、その一方、空欄の右側には breakdown という名詞にさまざまな語句が修飾語としてくっついて、名詞のはたらきをする大きなかたまりができあがっています。このような名詞のかたまりを「主語＋動詞」の文にくっつけることは、(C) の接続詞や (A) の副詞(句)ではできません。それができるのは、前置詞の後ろには必ず名詞（のはたらきをするかたまり）が入ることから、(句) 前置詞です。したがって、ここでは (B) と (D) から文意で (B) を選択します。

Chapter 15 Company Museums and Cafés

Vocabulary Questions

以下の語句の意味を、下の語群から選びましょう。

1. assemble　　_____
2. attractive　　_____
3. compare　　_____
4. disappointed　　_____
5. enthusiast　　_____
6. environmental　　_____
7. exciting　　_____
8. exhibit　　_____
9. expert　　_____
10. feature　　_____
11. in advance　　_____
12. origin　　_____
13. participate in　　_____
14. policy　　_____
15. product　　_____
16. recipe　　_____
17. registration　　_____
18. reservation　　_____
19. tip　　_____
20. various　　_____

こつ	予約	魅力的な	～に参加する
起源	専門家	さまざまな	～をくらべる
政策	調理法	前もって	～を展示する
製品	熱狂者	がっかりした	～を特集する
登録	環境の	わくわくする	～を組み立てる

Language in Use

Audio 2-13

音声を聴いて空欄を埋めましょう。さらに、完成した文の日本語訳を下線部に書きましょう。

1. Peter was the boss of the project, and he was treated (　　　)(　　　).

   _____

2. The banquet room has to be booked at least two weeks (　　　)(　　　).

   _____

3. This book is (　　　)(　　　) for students interested in the history of these companies.

   _____

Reading

🔊 Audio 2-14

1 Many companies in Japan have a place where the public can learn more about their products. Not only do they allow visitors to learn about the history of the companies, but also to try various products. Let's look at seven interesting places that you can visit to learn more. All of these
5 places are open to the public and do not require a reservation.

2 Somewhere you can learn more about the history of toilets, as well as plumbing in general, is the TOTO Museum in Fukuoka Prefecture. The museum not only exhibits many TOTO products, including the
10 world-famous "WASHLET™," but also provides information about its philosophy in manufacturing them, and about the culture and history of plumbing equipment. The museum itself was created based on the environmental policies of TOTO, and as such it features water saving technology, uses solar power, and was partially
15 constructed with recycled materials.

3 A very "hands-on" place to visit is the Yanmar Museum in Nagahama City, Shiga Prefecture. It was opened in 2013, to commemorate the company's 100th anniversary, in the birthplace of the company's
20 founder, Magokichi Yamaoka. Visitors to the museum  can see old diesel engines and learn more about the history of Yanmar and Mr. Yamaoka. Visitors can also operate machines such as a Yanmar digger or a pleasure boat. The museum is also very popular with children who can experience riding on a tractor or a combine harvester.

25 **4** If you are hungry, why not visit the Wood Egg Okonomiyaki Museum run by Otafuku Sauce Co.? There, you can learn about the company, and the history and culture of Okonomiyaki as well. Perhaps the most exciting experience is actually
30 cooking Okonomiyaki yourself at the museum, under the guidance and supervision of the experts. Although the museum is open to everyone, and you can enjoy the exhibits freely, you need to make a reservation to participate in the tour or cooking class. So, visit their website for registration in advance!

35 **5** For many people around the world, coffee is a part of daily life. A good way to find out more about coffee is to visit the UCC Coffee Museum on Port Island in Hyogo Prefecture, which was opened in 1987. In 2007, the company added the "UCC Coffee Academy" inside the museum. At the

museum and academy, people can learn about the origin and history of coffee, how it is cultivated and about different types of coffee. Information about roasting techniques is also available, as well as tips about the best ways to prepare and enjoy coffee. There is also a tasting corner so that visitors can compare different varieties.

6 Although you may have already visited the UCC museum, if you still feel like more coffee, you could visit Shimano Square in the Grand Front Osaka building in the center of Osaka. There is a café serving drinks and food where you can read many books about cycling and fishing. There are also galleries inside. In the Shimano Cycle Gallery, you can learn about the history of bicycles and also about the different components and how a bicycle is assembled. If you are more interested in fishing, you should check out the Shimano Fishing Gallery, where you can see the range of Shimano's fishing tackle, and even learn a new recipe for cooking fish each month.

7 To learn even more, you can visit the Bicycle Museum in Sakai City. The museum introduces the history of bicycles, and also regularly offers an opportunity for visitors to ride classic bikes. There are classes to help children who cannot ride a bike yet. With hundreds of amazing bicycles on display, this place is a must for cycling enthusiasts.

8 Not far from Shimano Square, you can find Mazda Brand Space Osaka. Although it may appear at first glance like a dealer's showroom, you can't actually buy a car here. This place is purely meant to offer opportunities for visitors to learn about Mazda cars, as well as to feel the company's brand concept. Along with a display of several cars, talks are often held with Mazda engineers and designers from Hiroshima, who were actually involved in developing recently launched cars. Visitors can talk with them freely and ask questions to learn more.

9 So, when you have some spare time, why not visit one of these attractive places? You won't be disappointed.

NOTES

◆ l. 49 Grand Front Osaka　大阪駅に隣接した複合商業施設　◆ l. 57 the Bicycle Museum in Sakai City　大阪府堺市にある自転車博物館。公益財団法人シマノ・サイクル開発センターが運営している。

Synonym Questions

以下の語句の同意語を選びましょう。単語の左側の数字はその語句が出てくる本文の段落番号です。

1. 1 various　　　　＿＿＿＿＿＿＿＿
2. 1 reservation　　＿＿＿＿＿＿＿＿
3. 2 exhibit　　　　＿＿＿＿＿＿＿＿
4. 4 guidance　　　＿＿＿＿＿＿＿＿
5. 4 participate in　＿＿＿＿＿＿＿＿
6. 5 tip　　　　　　＿＿＿＿＿＿＿＿
7. 6 assemble　　　＿＿＿＿＿＿＿＿
8. 7 enthusiast　　＿＿＿＿＿＿＿＿
9. 8 dealer　　　　＿＿＿＿＿＿＿＿
10. 9 spare　　　　＿＿＿＿＿＿＿＿

| booking | direction | free | retailer | construct |
| display | hint | different | fan | join |

 Questions & Answers

質問の答えとして正しいものを一つ選びましょう。

1. In which place can every visitor sample food or drink?
    (A) The café at Shimano Square
    (B) The UCC Coffee Museum
    (C) The Wood Egg Okonomiyaki Museum

2. In which place can visitors talk with the engineers and designers of the company?
    (A) Mazda Brand Space Osaka
    (B) The TOTO Museum
    (C) The Yanmar Museum

3. Which of the following can visitors NOT do?
    (A) Cook Okonomiyaki at the Wood Egg Okonomiyaki Museum
    (B) Learn how to ride a bike at the Bicycle Museum
    (C) Purchase a car at Mazda Brand Space Osaka

3 Comprehension Check

本文の内容に合うものを一つ選びましょう。

1. ①〜③段落に関して
   (A) People can visit these seven places if they book in advance.
   (B) The TOTO Museum reflects TOTO's policies about the environment.
   (C) The Yanmar Museum exhibits many Yanmar products, but visitors can't operate any of them.
   (D) The Yanmar Museum was opened on the occasion of the 100th anniversary of Magokichi's birth.

2. ④〜⑤段落に関して
   (A) At the UCC Coffee Museum, visitors can get some advice on how to make coffee well.
   (B) At the Wood Egg Okonomiyaki Museum, people can cook Okonomiyaki themselves, even without a reservation.
   (C) The UCC Coffee Museum was added inside the UCC Coffee Academy.
   (D) Visitors can sample only one kind of coffee at the UCC Coffee Museum.

3. ⑥〜⑨段落に関して
   (A) In the Shimano Cycle Gallery, children can learn how to ride a bicycle.
   (B) In the Shimano Fishing Gallery, visitors can learn new methods of preparing fish dishes.
   (C) Mazda Brand Space Osaka isn't a dealer's showroom, so Mazda's cars aren't on display.
   (D) The Bicycle Museum exhibits classic bikes, but visitors can't ride any of them.

Composition

あなたが興味をもっている企業についてホームページなどで事実を調べ、例文を参考にして以下の空欄にあてはまる語句を入れて、その企業の説明を英語でしてみましょう。参照する企業は、例文ごとに変えても、すべて同じ企業でもかまいません。

例1 Somewhere you can learn more about <u>the history of toilets</u>, as well as <u>plumbing in general</u>, is <u>the TOTO Museum</u> in <u>Fukuoka Prefecture</u>.
トイレの歴史や水まわり全般についてもっと学べる場所は、福岡県にあるTOTOミュージアムである。

企業名 _____
Somewhere you can learn more about (　　　), as well as
(　　　), is (　　　) in (　　　).

例2 The most exciting experience is actually <u>cooking Okonomiyaki yourself</u> at <u>the Wood Egg Okonomiyaki Museum</u> run by <u>Otafuku Sauce Co</u>.
最も楽しい体験は、オタフクソースが運営するWood Eggお好み焼館で、実際にお好み焼きづくりができることである。

企業名 _____
The most exciting experience is actually (　　　) at (　　　)
run by (　　　).

例3 <u>The Yanmar Museum</u> was opened in <u>2013</u> to <u>commemorate the company's 100th anniversary</u>.
ヤンマーミュージアムは2013年に会社創業100周年を記念してオープンした。

企業名 _____
(　　　) was opened in (　　　) to (　　　).

Chapter 15

Company Museums and Cafés

5 Completing Tables

ホームページなどで事実を調べて、以下の表を例にならって完成させましょう。そして、ぜひ実際にこれらの施設を訪問してみてください！

施設名	場所	開館時間	休館日	入館料
TOTOミュージアム	福岡県 北九州市 小倉北区	10:00~17:00	月曜 夏期休暇 年末年始	無料 団体要予約 (20名以上)
ヤンマーミュージアム				
Wood Egg お好み焼館				
UCCコーヒー博物館				
シマノスクエア				
自転車博物館サイクルセンター				
マツダブランドスペース大阪				

Company Museums and Cafés **125**

本書は日本出版著作権協会(JPCA)が委託管理する著作物です。複写(コピー)・複製、その他著作物の利用については、事前にJPCA(電話 03-3812-9424, e-mail:info@e-jpca.com)の許諾を得て下さい。なお、無断でコピー・スキャン・デジタル化等の複製をすることは著作権法上の例外を除き、著作権法違反となります。

■■ 著者紹介および分担 ■■

吉野成美（よしの・なるみ）
近畿大学経済学部教授
企画立案、協力企業との連絡、教科書本文の編集及び執筆、全章の校正

Justin Harris（ジャスティン・ハリス）
近畿大学経済学部教授
教科書本文の執筆、全章の校正、全章の英文チェック

井上　治（いのうえ・おさむ）
近畿大学経済学部教授
企画立案、全章の冒頭と章末の文法説明および練習問題の作成、全章の校正

Paul Leeming（ポール・リーミング）
近畿大学経済学部教授
教科書本文の執筆、全章の校正、全章の英文チェック

Outstanding Monozukuri Companies in Japan
知られざる日本の「ものづくり」企業の世界

2019年4月10日　初版第1刷発行
2025年4月1日　初版第6刷発行

著　者	吉野成美／Justin Harris／井上　治／Paul Leeming
発 行 者	森　信久
発 行 所	株式会社　松柏社 〒102-0072　東京都千代田区飯田橋1-6-1 TEL 03 (3230) 4813（代表） FAX 03 (3230) 4857 http://www.shohakusha.com e-mail: info@shohakusha.com
装　幀	小島トシノブ（NONdesign）
本文レイアウト	一柳　茂（株式会社クリエーターズユニオン）
印刷・製本	日経印刷株式会社

ISBN978-4-88198-744-5
略　　号 = 744

Copyright © 2019 by Narumi Yoshino, Justin Harris, Osamu Inoue, and Paul Leeming
本書を無断で複写・複製することを禁じます。
落丁・乱丁は送料小社負担にてお取り替え致します。